Comments on other *Amazing Stories* from readers & reviewers

"Tightly written volumes filled with lots of wit and humour about famous and infamous Canadians."

Eric Shackleton, *The Globe and Mail*

"The heightened sense of drama and intrigue, combined with a good dose of human interest is what sets Amazing Stories *apart."*

Pamela Klaffke, *Calgary Herald*

"This is popular history as it should be... For this price, buy two and give one to a friend."

Terry Cook, a reader from Ottawa, on ***Rebel Women***

"Glasner creates the moment of the explosion itself in graphic detail...she builds detail upon gruesome detail to create a convincingly authentic picture."

Peggy McKinnon, *The Sunday Herald,* on ***The Halifax Explosion***

"It was wonderful...I found I could not put it down. I was sorry when it was completed."

Dorothy F. from Manitoba on ***Marie-Anne Lagimodière***

"Stories are rich in description, and bristle with a clever, stylish realness."

Mark Weber, *Central Alberta Advisor,* on ***Ghost Town Stories II***

"A compelling read. Bertin...has selected only the most intriguing tales, which she narrates with a wealth of detail."

Joyce Glasner, *New Brunswick Reader,* on ***Strange Events***

"The resulting book is one readers will wa with all the women in their lives

Lynn Martel, *Rocky Mountain Outlook,* on ***W***

THE CANADIAN HORSE

AMAZING STORIES®

THE CANADIAN HORSE

The Fascinating Story of Canada's National Breed

Art Montague

HISTORY

James Lorimer & Company Ltd., Publishers
Toronto

James Lorimer & Company Ltd., Publishers acknowledges the support of the Ontario Arts Council. We acknowledge the financial support of the Government of Canada through the Canada Book Fund for our publishing activities. We acknowledge the support of the Canada Council for the Arts for our publishing program. We acknowledge the Government of Ontario through the Ontario Media Development Corporation's Ontario Book Initiative.

Canada Council
for the Arts

Library and Archives Canada Cataloguing in Publication

Montague, Art
The Canadian horse : the fascinating story of Canada's national breed / Art Montague.

(Amazing stories)
Issued also in an electronic format.
ISBN 978-1-55277-583-7

1. Canadian horse. I. Title. II. Series: Amazing stories (Toronto, Ont.)

SF293.C29M65 2010 636.1 C2010-902661-6

James Lorimer & Company Ltd., Publishers
317 Adelaide Street West, Suite 1002
Toronto, ON, Canada
M5V 1P9
www.lorimer.ca

Printed in Canada

Contents

Prologue

Ray Lalonde and his brother Gerry are horse breeders, trainers, and dealers with a farm outside Cumberland, Ontario.

Their farm, called Beckett's Creek, is unassumingly typical: rambling farm house, barns, equipment sheds, and a low building that serves as an office, tack room, and storage space. Nothing is special about this building—except for one wall, which is covered to the ceiling with award ribbons and framed presentation photos. The Lalondes' horses won these awards for embodying Canada's heritage.

The Lalondes' story begins in 1904 when their grandfather arrived in Cumberland with his family and a team of two work horses. The horses were of a special but well-known breed. By 1904 the breed had acquired a variety of names in English-speaking communities across much of North America. Often they were simply called "French Canadian" horses, but the breed was also known as "le canadien," "the Canadian," and "the little iron horse."

By any name, their reputation as all-purpose horses was well established. They could consistently outwork heavier horses in farm fields and forests. They could be ridden for pleasure or raced for profit. In harness, they could draw elegant carriages as willingly as they drew heavy freight

A foal at Hidden Meadow Farms, near Orton, Ontario.

wagons, stagecoaches, and Conestogas. Armies preferred them for hauling artillery and supply wagons, especially under fire. Hard-charging cavalry rode them into battle.

The Canadian breed, however, was prized for one other supremely important quality—it could improve other breeds. Indeed, it had contributed to the foundation of many other North American types, including the Morgan, the Standardbred, and the Tennessee Walking Horse.

Unfortunately, the Canadian was just too good, too

much in demand for crossbreeding. Alarmed by the decline in purebred Canadians, about the same time the Lalonde farm was being established, the Quebec government began a breeding program for "le petit cheval de fer." Ever so slowly the government's efforts did begin to pay off, but after World War I horsepower became motor power, gasoline replaced oats, and tractors replaced horses. The Canadian was on the trail to extinction.

Despite the modest success of the government program, the number of purebred Canadians had dwindled from an estimated high of some 150,000 in the middle of the nineteenth century to only about 400 in the 1970s. Bred uniquely in Canada from the seventeenth century on—and perhaps the first North American–bred domestic type—the Lalonde horses were a living historical treasure.

Fortunately, the Lalonde family and other breeders preserved the Canadian. Today, from a few hundred, the number of registered Canadians has increased to nearly 6,000. Not surprisingly, most of them are in Quebec, their home province. Others can be found across Canada, in some parts of the United States, and even a few in Europe.

Of the million horses in Canada, 6,000 is barely a handful. But no other breed can claim to be Canada's official national horse, an honour cast in federal legislation in 2002. Nor has any other horse breed or, for that matter, perhaps any other animal—not even the beaver—had a more influential role in shaping Canada from its earliest beginnings in New France and Acadia.

Ray and Gerry Lalonde are certainly aware of this history; they see the reasons for it every day in their barns and meadows. They see the horses' even temperament, quick intelligence, surprising strength, and willingness to take up any task. The Lalondes' horses are trained to both saddle and harness, as familiar with trail rides as with leisurely carriage jaunts around Ottawa's Parliament Buildings. Other Canadians compete in exhibitions and show rings across the country, from small local shows to the internationally famous Battle of the Breeds at Calgary's Spruce Meadows and Toronto's Royal Winter Fair.

Generally, Canada's history is embodied in architecture, statues, dusty texts, photos, and film. But the Canadian horse is very much alive, carrying history in its genes. That the Canadian could contribute so much to Canada for more than 300 years, while at times having to stave off extinction, is a measure of its ongoing durability and versatility. Perhaps these qualities go back to 1665, to the beginning; not in North America, but in the royal stables of King Louis XIV, the Sun King, when the ancestors of what became the Canadians were carefully selected to assist in the settlement of New France.

Chapter 1 Coming Through Hell

Just what constitutes a horse breed seems a fair question.

In the beginning, what became the Canadian horse breed was simply a composite developed by crossbreeding Norman and Breton horses. Purists might argue that the Normans and Bretons had Friesian, Arab, and Andalusian blood—which they did—as well as the genes of European woods ponies. As a further complication, in the distant past a distinctive Breton breed didn't even exist: Bretons, so-called, were simply horses that had been bred in the province of Brittany.

"Breed" is a term applied to domestic animals. Breeds

are identified as "animals that, through selection and breeding, have come to resemble one another and pass those traits uniformly to their offspring."

In his book *The Genetics of Population*, Dr. Jay L. Lush was hard-pressed to define "breed." He finally concluded the following:

> *A breed is a group of domestic animals, termed as such by common consent of breeders...a term which arose among breeders of livestock...one might say, for their own use, and no one is warranted in assigning to this word a scientific definition...it is their word, and the breeders' common usage is what we must accept as the correct definition.*

Certainly the Canadian satisfies this definition as a "breed," but in these attempts at definition is a suggestion that breeds are deliberately developed by livestock breeders and users. Indeed, many were and still are. But on this point the Canadian horse departs. In the critical early years in New France, habitant horse breeders were not solely responsible for directing breed development. Through natural selection, the horses mostly did it on their own.

Later, when the colonies were more secure and horse

numbers increased, settlers could begin breeding their horses for specific purposes. To that extent the horses were purpose-bred.

Today the car in the driveway tells something about its owner. The BMW, Cadillac, Mercedes, or Lexus indicates solid success. Corvettes, Porsches, and Lamborghinis suggest the success has some flair to it. Then there's the drab five- or six-year-old workaday sedan or minivan, wearied by morning commutes, trips to the mall, and children's pickup and delivery services. Other vehicles have very little to do with status—the eighteen-wheelers, dump trucks, half-tons, cargo vans, tanks, armoured personnel carriers, and so forth.

Before motorized vehicles were invented, horses fulfilled all of these roles, and similarly implied something about the people who used them.

For example, Genghis Khan's Mongols bred fast, resilient horses, used them in the conquest of much of Asia and Europe, and then galloped them over the longest "pony express" routes in history to provide the communication links that held the Mongol empire together. These tough little horses weren't equine Rolls Royces, but they were economic and military mainstays.

The records suggest, though, that the Romans did have the Rolls Royces. One was a white stallion named Incinatus, owned by the Emperor Caligula. Although Caligula is said to have been less than sane, he unquestionably revered

"Habitant Sleigh, View Near the Canadian Line," painting by Cornelius Krieghoff c. 1847.

Incinatus. Caligula built his horse a marble stable with ivory veneer throughout. The manger was of solid ivory. Eighteen servants were assigned to attend the horse's needs, one of whom was to ensure the horse's oats were laced with gold flakes. Rumour had it that Caligula actually appointed Incinatus to the Roman Senate.

Despite his excesses, Caligula may have been a good judge of horses, perhaps rivalling France's King Louis XIV, popularly known as The Sun King. During his reign, the longest in the history of France, and, indeed, of Europe, Louis moulded France's golden age, and his horses were part of it.

The golden age was mostly about Louis's vanity. On that his biographers agree. To him, ceremony and pomp were celebrations of royal prerogatives, as was an enlightened, cultured court. Louis became France's foremost patron of the arts—of painting, sculpture, literature, music, and architecture. For each he established academies, to nurture and reward the best artists of the country. His academy of architecture was the foundation for the design of the Paris Observatory and his palace at Versailles is still the symbol of France's then-greatness in the world.

The Versailles complex is one of the most magnificent achievements of the era, and much of it still stands today. Tourists exclaim over the palace itself, and over the meticulously landscaped splendour of the gardens, designed by the brilliant Le Nôtre. But tourists do not often notice the Epicure, the 600-horse stable Louis ordered constructed to house many of the best horses known in Europe at that time.

Although the Epicure was not started until 1679, by 1665 Louis was already assembling and breeding horses at Versailles. Unlike many of the king's expenditures, which were often seen as extravagant personal indulgences, the horses were seen as a necessity. Louis regularly embroiled France in wars with his European neighbours, and his ground forces—infantry, cavalry, and artillery—relied on horses. At the same time, France was expanding its colonial possessions in North America and the Caribbean; the colonies also required horses.

During the mid-1660s, furs and fish from New France were important revenue sources. Louis wanted to strengthen this economic base by encouraging more emigration to the colonies and by increasing the colonies' agricultural capacity.

In 1665 and 1666 a census of New France (which then included present-day Quebec, the Maritime provinces, and a considerable part of northern New York state, the New England states, and Ohio), counted 3,215 habitants, clergy, and nobles; but men outnumbered women almost two to one. Realizing that farms required families to be successful, Louis decreed that 700 marriageable women between the ages of fifteen and thirty years were to be persuaded to emigrate to New France. By then his advisors had also convinced him that horses would be required if farming were to thrive. Until then the habitants had been making do with dogs and a few oxen. As a spinoff, said his advisors, the horse trade itself might hold some potential profits for his treasury.

At that time, the only horses in the colony were a handful imported solely for the nobles and high church officials, the first one having arrived from France in 1647 for the use of the Governor, Charles Huault de Montmagny. These horses were for transportation—no thought was given to breeding them.

Nearly two decades later, by the time of the census,

much had changed in the colony, and the king struck a deal with New France's gentry. In effect, he would sell them the foundation stock they required to begin breeding horses. In turn, they could sell the offspring to their habitant settlers. With luck, enough horses would be bred to also supply France's military needs in the colony and, of course, the needs of the clergy.

Selecting the appropriate stock had to be done carefully, but Louis had many horses and breeds from which to choose. He knew New France to be a savage land; thickly forested, rocky, sometimes swampy, and unblessed by temperate weather. The horses he had in his stables were first-rate, but they were used to pampering. Warm stalls and blankets were their norm. So too were regular exercise and meticulous grooming, plus plenty of oats, sweet hay, fresh water, and a daily change of bedding straw. But the horses he eventually selected for New France were of breeds that might manage, if not thrive, in the unforgiving environment.

Brittany and Normandy were the two French provinces to which the king turned for his selection. The Breton horse was small, hardy, and energetic, with a reputation as a good worker. The Normans were a strain developed from interbreeding with Spanish Andalusians and Dutch Friesians. The Normans were almost the same size as the Bretons but had longer tails and manes. For many, their tails would grow to touch the ground. The Normans were also known as excellent trotters. This would make them a choice as riding horses, and even for cavalry use. They also did well in carriage service, either singly or as part of a team.

Breton and Norman horses came from the areas in France where the climate and the terrain were as nearly like those in the new colony as the king could find at hand. He knew that hardiness would be critical.

So, on the sixteenth of July 1665 the French merchant ship *Marie-Thérèse* tied up to the wharf at Quebec City. Carefully, crew and longshoremen led fourteen horses up from the ship's hold and onto the dock. It was the first solid ground the twelve mares and two stallions had felt beneath their hooves for more than nine weeks.

Their voyage across the Atlantic had begun on May 10 from the French port of Le Havre. It had started with twenty mares. That eight of these tough little horses had died en route is a measure of the perils of transatlantic crossings in those days.

The *Marie-Thérèse*'s time at sea was about average. At between 250 and 300 tons, the ship's size was about average, too. For the horses, nothing was average. They would have been crammed in the hold, tied in makeshift stalls, probably hobbled, and likely in darkness most of the time. Forget exercise and daily grooming; they would have been fortunate to have their stalls periodically cleaned and fresh straw bedding laid. Their diet may have started with fresh oats, hay, and water. By journey's end, remaining oats would be mouldy, the hay sour, and the water brackish. Indeed, though they could not realize it, these horses probably would never taste oats again.

The comparatively tiny wooden ship would have jostled with every swell, and the swells were constant. Moreover, the North Atlantic Ocean in summer has its share of storms, especially in the clash of currents and weather systems churning near Newfoundland and in the Gulf of St. Lawrence. Rising and plunging in heavy seas, the ship would have shuddered, creaked, and grated, every joint straining to stay together, sails slack then instantly taut, snapping in the wind...and all of that echoing like hammers to the helpless horses. For the seamen the voyage would have been arduous, certainly perilous, but nothing most of them hadn't experienced before. For the horses it would have been such hell as to make New France seem a paradise.

Chapter 2
Culture Shock

A settler's life in early seventeenth-century New France was usually brutal and always dangerous. Most settlers were reliant on the fur trade and the summer supply ships from France. Any farming was little more than a scratching out of small garden plots that the Natives would often destroy before they could be harvested. Even among the elite, near-starvation and disease were common during the long winters.

The French government tried to encourage settlement and growth of farming in New France by providing favoured nobles and clergy with vast land grants. Unfortunately, these were mostly rock and virgin forest. As well, most of the grantees, comfortable in France, chose to leave their land undeveloped, treating it as a potential long-term investment rather than as an immediate opportunity.

Louis XIV decided enough was enough. He rescinded many of the land grants and extended France's seigneurial system of landholding to the colony. Now a seigneur had to live on his land and develop it to keep it. Each seigneur was also obligated to build a school and a church. To help this initiative along, the king also arranged shipments of seed and farm implements to New France.

These were big steps forward, but would work only if the settlements were secure. Security could come only if the annual Iroquois threat was neutralized.

For years, as soon as the ice melted from the rivers and lakes and the high waters of spring runoff had subsided, Iroquois war parties had come north to raid the settlers and the settlers' Algonquin allies. Defending against them left the colonists little time to clear and seed land. Indeed, most settlers chose to stay very close to the safety of the forts.

During the summer of 1665, seven ships arrived from France and the French colonial island of Martinique in the Caribbean, bringing more than 1,200 infantry troops and their officers. It was the Carignan-Salières Regiment, including seasoned veterans who had fought the previous year against formidable armies in Turkey. Undoubtedly, they could clear out the Iroquois in quick time. In New France, however, all their previous experience wouldn't mean much.

No sooner had they built a few small forts and settled

in when a new colonial governor, Daniel de Courcelle, eager to gain the King's favour, ordered the Carignan-Salières to attack at once. But it was the middle of winter. Even the Iroquois avoided winter warfare.

Nevertheless, and in spite of the regimental commander's misgivings, a battle group of approximately 300 troops and 200 colonial militia (settlers who had volunteered for service) set out from Quebec in January 1666, picked up more volunteers at Montreal, and headed for the Dutch settlement of Schenectady, far to the south in what is now New York State, to teach the Iroquois a lesson.

This expedition was a disaster. The troops froze in the forests, they didn't have proper winter equipment, and when they got to Schenectady they were so exhausted that the Iroquois attacked them, killing several men. The survivors struggled back to Quebec, with more of them lost along the way. As soon as the ice went out, the Iroquois raids resumed.

But in late summer the French mounted another assault against the Iroquois, and this time they were successful. Raiding at harvest time, they destroyed the Iroquois' crops of corn, beans, and squash, the "three sisters" of Iroquois legend that were the tribe's dietary staples. They also put the Iroquois' principal villages to the torch.

In 1667, severely weakened, the Iroquois tribal chiefs sought peace and a treaty was signed. This defeat allowed the

French to continue colonizing Quebec in safety.

Its mission completed, the Regiment was ordered back to France, but its members were given a tempting option. Officers and soldiers who wished to stay and settle were offered generous land grants under the seigneurial system. Of a force of 1,200, about a third elected to stay, providing the colony with both a potential nucleus of farmers and a group of experienced soldiers who might volunteer for the militia.

By itself, the fur trade could not economically support the colonies. Louis XIV and his advisors decided to augment the trade with a stable and flourishing agricultural base. Louis was already regularly shipping in supplies of seed and livestock such as poultry, sheep, and cattle (none of which thrived particularly well). He also arranged for single women of marriageable age to emigrate to the colony, hoping to establish families. To keep the men at work on the farms, rather than have them prospecting far off into the bush, the king placed restrictions on fur trading. Most importantly, he provided a foundation stock of horses.

Without horses, farming would have languished far below the level of self-sufficiency, and the colonies would have stayed dependent upon imports from France. With horses, eventually, the habitants managed to harvest enough grain even to export small amounts back to the mother country. Most farm products, though, were consumed by the habitants and their families, and most surplus was sold in the

Four Canadians pulling the plough at West Gimlet Farms.

colonial centres, such as Quebec and Montreal.

Between 1665 and 1670 the horses sent to New France remained the property of the government, except for two mares and a stallion given to the Ursuline religious order in 1667.

Intendant Jean Talon distributed these horses among the seigneurs, most of whom were minor nobility, and to former military officers and clergy. He charged 100 livres or one foal per year for three years. At the end of three years the "renter" would own the horse. Of course, if ill befell the horse during that time, the renter was still liable. Colts used for rent payments were maintained by the government until they too could be rented to seigneurs. In their turn, the seigneurs rented horses to their habitant tenants, and the whole system became quite lucrative as the number of horses multiplied.

By 1679 the horse population in New France had grown to 145. In 1698, it was 684. Horse breeding may have been the most successful aspect of the king's ambitious plan for farming in the colony, for in other ways the habitants were not doing well. Although the land along the St. Lawrence was fertile, it had to be cleared and labour was in short supply. Having the horses did speed the clearing and ploughing, but the growing season was too short for many of the crops the habitants tried to grow. (Ironically, today, after much experimentation in crop selection, the land in southwestern Quebec and southeastern Ontario is second only to the prairie grain belt in fertility and crop yields.)

The colony was settling into relative peace. The descendants of the king's horses continued to thrive, so much so that in 1709 the Montreal settlement decreed that farmers would be limited to two horses and one foal, with the surplus being sent to slaughter. The habitants ignored the law. The horses continued to multiply; they were already an integral part of New France society.

By providing horses for New France, the king's plan was on the mark. The first horses in the colony had been selected for characteristics his advisors believed would enable them to survive the rigors of primitive colonial life and contribute to progress. These characteristics included strength, stamina, and an even temperament, compressed into a small physical build. They had to be horses that could adapt to all seasons, however inhospitable, and perform in all roles.

"All roles" meant something more than providing labour. These horses were to be more than workers. They would serve the military, pace with dignity, and—when harnessed to carriages—demonstrate the elegance expected by the gentry.

At that time no single breed in Europe possessed all of these qualities, but some people had thought that Norman and Breton horses, if interbred, might develop most of them. What occurred in New France far exceeded most experts' hopes, and led eventually to the Canadian breed as it is known today.

The most important factor in the creation of the Canadian was more accidental than planned. By choice and geography, the French settlements along the St. Lawrence and, to a lesser extent, those in maritime Acadia, were isolated.

Waterways were still the main transportation arteries in northeastern North America during the last half of the seventeenth and first decades of the eighteenth centuries. Horses were important only where there were settlements; that is, where farming was taking place or where significant trade centres were being established. In those regards, the British colonies south of New France were far more developed.

During the same period colonial expansion was high on the agenda of many European powers, notably France, England, Spain, and Holland, all of which had staked territorial claims in North America and the Caribbean. The rivalry between France and England over New World territorial issues and European political issues often burst into warfare. These conditions effectively isolated New France on the continent; which, of course, meant the horses were isolated too.

Apparently the horses didn't mind isolation a bit. The first horses quickly shook off their horrendous sea voyage and the shock of discovering that they were now obliged to labour in a new environment, to say nothing of having to feed themselves, right down to scrounging for their own food. There was no one to exercise them or to brush them down daily. There was no one to clean their stalls—most of them had no stalls.

Empty bellies rumbling, the horses quickly learned to forage along the marshy riverbanks and in the brush that still covered most of the narrow strips of seigneurial land that stretched back from the banks. Lucky horses found patches of wild meadow grass where half-hearted attempts had been made to clear the land and to sow crops.

Warding off clouds of blackflies and mosquitoes was

another matter. Within a few generations the horses had grown their now-characteristic long, thick manes to protect their necks and heads.

They also grew tails that could reach the ground, perfect for swishing away bothersome insects. Unfortunately, docking those tails was an accepted habitant custom in those times, which meant cutting off the tail skirts that would have been so effective against bugs. To the habitants, docking was not only necessary for the sake of appearance, but prevented the tail from becoming tangled in carriage or plough harnesses. For the horses, expected to live outdoors during all seasons, including winter, the practice was simply another obstacle to overcome or to tolerate. When not called on for their labour, to escape clouds of insects in summer the horses would often simply shelter in the densest bush they could find.

Strong hooves were another characteristic the horses developed as generations of foals were born. Most of these horses lived their lives unshod where a cracked hoof could cripple, a fate that would as often as not lead to the horse's being put down by the owner. Often there were no blacksmiths or farriers in the colony with the skill to shoe horses.

With wilderness for their home the horses became very sure-footed, able to move safely and gracefully across all types of terrain. The wilderness was not a challenge for their strength and stamina. Day in and day out, the horses could haul logs, pull up tree stumps, and drag stone boats piled with hundreds of pounds of rocks dug out during land clearing. With their help, more land could be cleared in a week than a settler alone could clear in a season. The change in the landscape of New France was dramatic.

Many early settlers had never before farmed or even worked with horses, but the horses were amazingly tolerant toward them. They found their own food and shelter. Often the mares foaled alone in the bush. Yet, in harness, the horses were easy to train, patient, and gentle, ready to respond whatever the task. No wonder that Canadians became known as "easy keepers."

Chapter 3
Growing Fame

In appearance and temperament the Canadian became a distinctive, recognizable breed. By the early eighteenth century the Canadian was as familiar in the New France countryside as the habitant farmer and his family. Their numbers exceeded a thousand in the Quebec colonies and they were becoming just as valuable in France's maritime colonies.

By the standards and circumstances of the times the horses were treated reasonably well. To be sure, they had no hay to eat but straw was available, though far less nourishing or tasty. Almost every habitant homestead had a loft built onto or near the house, where straw was stored. Beyond straw the horses were on their own, but the shape of the habitant farms supported their foraging.

The farms were narrow strips of land with one end fronting on a riverbank or lakeshore. These shorelines were usually marshy, unsuitable for farming, yet providing edible reeds and swamp grass. Where forest had been cleared or culled for timber, meadowlands or light second-growth bush provided more vegetation. On some seigneurial holdings, a community meadow was set aside for grazing. Here everyone's horses could herd and, not incidentally, breed, and they were easily accessible when required.

During winter, the working horses had to rely on the habitant's straw supply, which first went to his other livestock. Colts were left to self-forage, with the habitants taking the view that this toughened them up. During this period the colonies were trying to establish beef and dairy cattle but, due to the harsh climate, with limited success. The horses managed by browsing on any scrub brush that might be poking through the snow and whatever vegetation they could uncover by scraping snow away. They also developed a taste for tree bark, which some Canadians still favour to this day.

The winter work pace for the horses could be fierce but it was sporadic. Winter was logging season, when habitants would go into the bush to cut timber for housing, fencing, and firewood. The horses would skid out the logs, sometimes to a river's edge. They did this through belly-high snow and unbroken bush, with rocks and deadfalls sometimes beneath their hooves. The habitants relied on the horses to pick the safest path. But they were not hauling out one log at a time. Sledges would be piled high, horses teamed in pairs, one in front of the other. If one horse should falter (a rarity) the stronger would haul both the weaker horse and the load.

The emerging breed was intelligent and willing to work but not always prepared to put aside self-interest. Even under harness, a wise horse might feign lameness just long enough to nibble up some dried berries peeping through the snow by the side of a tangled, dangerous track. One misstep could mean a split hoof on a sharp rock, a leg broken between boulders, or, worse, a plummet into the treacherous entanglement of roots and branches left when trees have been uprooted during storms, sheared by lightning strikes, or heaped along shorelines by floods. Still, the horses worked inexhaustibly, and they thrived.

By the mid-eighteenth century, the few dozen horses had become hundreds. They became so plentiful and so adept at foraging food that other livestock, such as cattle, were going short. Government officials in Montreal tried several times to limit the number of horses allowed in each household, hoping to give the cattle a better chance because, generally, people would prefer to eat beef rather than horsemeat, but all those efficient horses were making it harder to establish a beef industry. Even General Montcalm expressed concern that his troops were restive because of their horsemeat diet. But legislating numbers of horses turned out to be rather like legislating Prohibition; it didn't work. And the cattle production program was not going well anyway. Apart from the horses competing for forage, the climate was hard on cattle. Their birth rates were low, their survival rates lower, and the beasts that did make it were thin, stringy, and hardy—and hardly tasty.

Before horses were available, travel had been by small, dog-drawn wagons. Heavy farm work had been done by oxen, which were not particularly suited to the habitants' small landholdings and required considerable care. A light, self-sufficient work horse was perfect, and that was the Canadian.

On average standing fourteen to sixteen hands high (one hand equals four inches), the Canadians' short stature was deceptive, belying their exceptional power. Eager to serve, patient, intelligent, and self-sufficient as they adapted, these horses became almost too good to be true.

Their excellence as workhorses alone would have been enough to secure their reputation, but the Canadian proved to be much more than a workhorse. With the surplus of horses, some standouts were turned to purposes other than hard labour.

Some were trained for riding. Commonly they would carry children to school and menfolk to visits with neighbours or to the settlements to conduct business. Or, as often as not, they might simply be ridden for pleasure.

Others were used exclusively to draw carriages and sleighs, and became vital year-round for getting the families to church and to events such as weddings, dances, and other social gatherings. Having horses enabled the settlers to maintain closer contact with each other, transforming a scattering of isolated settlers into cohesive communities.

As reliance on the Canadians increased, opportunities for specialized trades emerged—blacksmithing, harness making, saddlery, and carriage building.

More successful settlers were now able to use some of their horses for even more specialized purposes. One of these was horse racing, which became a passion throughout New France.

Riding in preference to walking is not something that appeared with the automobile. In rural Quebec the preference was to "Harness up the horse." The horses weren't used only for useful work, nor only for business; the settlers simply loved to go calling on their neighbours.

The arrangement of the farms, each stretching in a narrow strip inland from the waterways, made visiting easy. From offshore, on the river, from Montreal to Trois-Rivières and along the St. Lawrence's north shore, the close-set farms looked like one long, uninterrupted village of whitewashed cabins, barns, and livestock pens, suggesting a population far denser than actually lived there.

As well, the settlers living between Quebec and

Montreal had a roadway, le Chemin du Roi, a through-route ploughed out along the shoreline during the 1730s. In some places the road was seven metres wide, with sturdy wooden bridges, fords over streams, and ferries where necessary. While theoretically the road was open year-round, travelling on the river ice was preferred in winter. Even in other seasons, weather permitting, boats were the popular choice. Nevertheless, with horses proliferating and shorter cross roads branching from le Chemin du Roi, land transport rose in importance.

Daily life for the settlers from the seventeenth to the mid nineteenth century may have seemed harsh, certainly by modern Canadian standards—unrelenting hard work just to stay alive. And, during the early years, it unquestionably was harsh; but compared to the lives of the poor classes in France it was life in the Garden of Eden.

In France, arable land was scarce and those working it were mercilessly exploited by the upper classes. Moving to the cities for employment was not much of an option. The cities were overcrowded, filthy, and thick with disease. The nation's economy was being drained to finance wars and to construct monumental civil works, such as Versailles. In the cities the danger of conscription into the king's armies was higher than in the countryside, and that could mean separation from one's family for many years. The gaps between rich and poor, royal and rabble, powerful and powerless were huge. The opportunity to move upward from one class to another was blocked at every turn.

New France was different. Land was abundant. Opportunities were measured by personal energy and ambition. Mutual needs such as sustenance and security blurred class lines. Despite the initial primitive conditions, industry was rewarded and the settlers slowly shaped an economic and social life well suited to the colonies. That included owning a horse, or many. In New France anyone could own a horse; in Mother France, horses were the preserve of the gentry—nobles, merchants, and clergy. In New France, if one were buying a horse, terms were available, "on approved credit," as they are now when we buy cars.

Horses knit the colony together, enabling a quality and style of life for everyone that would have been impossible in the old country. Work went easier and faster. The settlers could satisfy their social obligations, not least those to the church, which in most respects was more powerful than the civil authority. Its calendar was crowded with special celebrations, festivals, and holidays at which attendance was almost mandatory. Religious observance required far more than mere regular attendance on Sundays.

Journals written during those times record several occasions when civil officials responsible for economic well-being requested that the church reduce its number of "events," because they occupied so much time when the farmers needed to be working the fields. Officials argued that economic development was being impeded. The church shrugged off these pleas—spiritual growth was far more important.

Habitants had no lack of engagements. Michaelmas, Christmas, New Year's, Easter, and Mayday were important. An abundance of saints had to be celebrated. Church attendance on Sundays was *de rigueur,* if only because after services any new civil proclamations, including those from the king, plus other news, would be read out to the gathering. Then, of course, there were weddings, communions, and funerals—more than a few, because the habitants usually had large families.

Just as we have civic holidays today, at least once a month the settlers had a community holiday—berrying, flax-beating, corn husking, and harvest home (bringing the last wagonload from the fields) among them—and each one was a time for a festival. Any breaks in the social schedule were quickly filled with impromptu parties and visits among neighbours. By horseback and by horse-drawn sleigh, carriage, and cart, parishioners and their families could get to these events; and the festivities—sometimes fuelled by the copious supply of brandy from Mother France—often carried on into the wee hours. Then, too, there was the horse racing. If the settlers had one heady passion, horse racing was it. Pedestrians walking to or from church had to learn to be

"Sleigh Race on the St. Lawrence at Quebec" by Cornelius Krieghoff, 1852.

nimble. Racing was so prevalent in some districts that efforts were made to ban it on the trails near churches.

Racing apart, habitants typically drove their horses fast, hard, and relentlessly. In winter, it was common to see a horse being driven flat out for ten or twelve miles, then—sweated and ice-glazed—being left to wait unsheltered in the subzero elements for hours while the owner socialized or attended an "event." The conventional attitude was that this toughened the horse and made the breed stronger.

Daily habitant life is recorded in the paintings of a famous Dutch-born artist named Cornelius Krieghoff. They are a priceless graphic record of the time, and his outdoor scenes almost always include *les chevaux Canadiens.*

One memorable painting, "Run off the Road in a Blizzard," shows a toppled sleigh, its driver shaking his fist at the departing "villain," while a helper thigh-deep in snow tries to quiet the victim's agitated horse. The "villain" is seen in the comfort of his own sleigh, looking back at the chaos he created, while his own horse dutifully treats the entire business as commonplace. Looking at the painting, one may wonder which of the two drivers was the speedster.

The sleighs in Krieghoff's paintings are of three designs. A popular one was flat like a toboggan with a wooden guardrail about waist-high. The driver and passengers rode standing. This was a particular favourite for ice racing. A second type was shaped like a large wooden box. In this the driver and passengers could hunker out of the wind, cozy under thick fur robes and rugs. This type was also useful for transporting large loads, such as firewood. The third was a "family sleigh," closer in design to the sleigh usually portrayed as transporting Santa Claus. This was high in the front and back, open on the sides, containing relatively high seats for passengers. It was like an open carriage with runners rather than wheels. The habitants were quite willing to race any of these types. So were the horses.

Krieghoff also captured for posterity the habitants' penchant for partying, and he did it even without showing the party itself. "Breaking up of a Country Ball, Early Morning," completed in 1857, subtitled "The Morning after a Merrymaking

"Breaking up of a Country Ball in Canada, Early Morning (The Morning After a Merrymaking in Lower Canada)" by Cornelius Krieghoff, 1857.

in Lower Canada," depicts the guests leaving just as the sun comes up. Central to the subject is a scene worthy of a Driving Under the Influence citation: a box-style sleigh on its side, passengers thrown helter-skelter on the snow-covered ground in the farmyard, and the horse, apparently uninjured, still standing attached in the harness. Other leave-takers are already in the saddle or in sleighs ready to go, and the host and hostess are on the veranda with some first-to-arrive–last-to-go roisterers: in all, an obviously happy departure for everybody, mishap notwithstanding. The horses, like those in most of Krieghoff's habitant paintings, are unmistakably Canadians.

While the habitants' treatment of their horses may seem

callous by today's standards, in reality they were regarded almost as family members. In 1757 during the siege of Montreal, with food running out, the governor ordered that horses be slaughtered. The protests were so strong—owners likening what was being proposed to cannibalism—that the official backed down. Shortly after, the settlement capitulated to the British.

The Seven Years War, which ran from 1756 to 1763, did not interrupt exports of the Canadians. "The French Horse," as the Canadian had come to be known in the northern states, remained popular, especially in New England. As well, the horse was common in what had been the French possessions in New York State, Michigan, and Illinois, and as far west as Minnesota.

After 1763 the north-south corridors, the natural commerce routes, opened wide and horses were regularly sold to dealers from the south. Montreal became a thriving market place for the horse trade. Among the more prominent dealers prior to the American Revolution was the later-to-be-infamous Benedict Arnold, who regularly brought manufactured goods from the south to trade for horses at Montreal. The horses would be herded back across the ice of Lake Champlain, often to be re-sold in New York City or Boston, some being shipped to the West Indies to work in the sugar cane fields. By the time the southern traders began working through the horse market at Montreal, New

France traders were already doing the same from the port of St. John's—selling their horses to sugar cane growers on the French-held islands in the Caribbean. Indeed, even very recently an Ontario breeder of Canadians, who happened to be holidaying in Martinique, was struck by the similarity between the horses still in use on that island and today's Canadians; they are practically indistinguishable.

The Americans expanded this trade, and soon Canadians were in use in St. Lucia, Cuba, Haiti, and Jamaica.

By 1775, when the American Revolution began, a firm pattern of trading in Canadian horses had been established. After the Revolution, another market opened when Loyalists who had fled north began settling in Upper Canada. They quickly discovered that Canadians from the St. Lawrence Valley were far superior for farming purposes to the horses they had brought with them.

As a workaday horse in Upper Canada, the Canadian was ideal. And their prepotence—their ability to pass on their characteristics even through crossbreeding—made them valuable breeders. Like the habitants, the Loyalists found that a small Canadian stallion bred with a larger mare usually produced a larger horse that retained the strength, stamina, and temperament of the Canadian. Indeed, breeders in Lower Canada bred a specific strain known as St. Lawrences, a somewhat heavier horse than the original Canadian but able to handle more demanding work in the logging industry.

Soon horses with Canadian blood were a substantial majority in Upper Canada, taking on a key role in the development of that region, just as their ancestors had in New France.

The horse trade with Americans continued after the Revolution, though it became less "public." The political friction in British-American relations meant little when there was a deal was to be done. The breeders in Lower Canada often had relatives still living south of the border and, in most cases, they still chafed at British rule.

For New Englanders, the Canadians had two attractions. First, they could tirelessly travel long distances under harness while requiring minimal upkeep. The numerous stagecoach and freight lines in New England preferred them. Second, Canadians were valued for their pacing ability. Pacers do not gallop. Rather, their gait is maintained by moving legs on one side of their body in unison. The Canadian pacers were very fast at this type of gait, and took readily to training.

The source of this talent may have been in the breed's Norman roots, or (as some believe) it may have resulted from crossbreeding with Rhode Island's Narragansett Pacer before the Narragansett became extinct. While a few Narragansetts may have been brought north, habitants had been favouring pacing horses over trotters for many years before the Rhode Island horses would have arrived on the scene—though certainly these Pacers, if crossbred with Canadians, would have enhanced the Canadians' pacing abilities. Possibly confirming this crossbreed, a specific strain known as the Canadian Pacer did emerge to dominate racing events along the eastern seaboard for decades. Historically, then, Canadian pacers have had considerable influence. The habitants and their Canadians are considered to be the founders of harness racing in North America, and this has since become an industry worth a billion dollars a year.

During the nineteenth century, the Canadian reached its height of influence throughout North America. Because it continued to be the best all-purpose horse, its genetic footprint spread exponentially.

Chapter 4
The Morgan: Cousin to the Canadian

The most famous and most historically important horse in the United States is the Morgan. While most Americans consider the Morgan a uniquely American breed, many breeders of Canadians north of the border argue that the Morgan is simply an American version of its northern neighbour.

They are annoyed that credit is rarely given to the Canadian as the breed behind the Morgan when, they believe, credit is definitely due. History does offer some compelling, though circumstantial, evidence in support of the northern viewpoint. For example, canny Yankee horse traders were known to purchase Canadians at Montreal and Quebec

City, then take them south and sell them to unsuspecting Americans as Morgans. The horses were so similar that even experts could be fooled.

Trade was brisk because Canadians were cheap and plentiful and Morgans were higher priced and in high demand. A Canadian selling for $20 in Quebec could easily be passed off as a Morgan and fetch $60 south of the border. The practice was so prevalent that Morgan breeders appealed to the authorities to stop the trade, but stopping the trade would have been very difficult. A Canadian owner would only have had to hitch a team to a buggy or to saddle up and ride across the border, and, as part of a prearranged deal, drive or ride non-Canadian horses back home to the north.

Nevertheless, the introduction of Canadians to the genetic mix that created the Morgan had started years before such sharp horse dealers began passing off Canadians. Canadians had long been available in the northeastern states, for example, because they were the horse of choice for the many stagecoach lines operating there.

The Morgan breed is considered by equine historians to have begun in 1789 when a foal named Figure was sired by a stallion named True Briton to a mare of inconclusive origin. The mare could well have been a Canadian or Canadian crossbreed, because by then Canadians were common in New England. Figure was owned by Justin Morgan, a Massachusetts farmer, horse breeder, and town official. Like many New Englanders of the time, Morgan wore many occupational hats.

In 1787, one of Morgan's hats was that of local tax collector. Through no fault of his own, he wasn't very good at it. Local people were going through hard times. They simply couldn't pay.

Normally, one might think, the government would lay claim to the delinquent taxpayers' property or at least charge some interest on the arrears. Not in Massachusetts. There, if taxes were uncollected or uncollectible, the tax collector was responsible for paying them. In January 1788, the state hauled Morgan into court, where he was ordered to pay the shortfall he had been unable to collect.

By the end of March that year Morgan had sold off his property and moved to Randolph, Vermont, taking along the mare that had been bred to True Briton.

Figure, the resulting colt, was a relatively small horse but he had stamina, strength, and speed.

New Englanders shared their Quebecois neighbours' love of horse racing, and Figure soon achieved a reputation in Vermont as a winner. In 1736 two well-known race horses from New York were making the rounds of the New England states, up against all comers for cash stakes. When they came to the town of Brookfield, close by Randolph, they were put up against Figure, and the little stallion left them in his dust. There were no million-dollar purses to be won in those days, and Justin Morgan took home a fifty-dollar prize, but to this day the stretch of road used for that memorable race is known as "the Morgan Mile." A few years later, Figure's great-grandson Ethan Allen 50 was considered to be the world's fastest trotting stallion.

Figure was much more than a racehorse. He also successfully competed in pulling contests, usually out-pulling heavy draft horses. And he was a hard worker. No idle time in the barn for him! Like Canadians, he was worked in fields and required to haul more than his share of logs from the bush, again outperforming heavier horses. Before his working career was done, Figure also served as a carriage and a riding horse. His strength and stamina became as legendary as his speed.

Figure could race and he could work. By themselves these qualities would have secured his reputation. Both pale, however, against his prepotence as a stud, which is considered to be the foundation of the Morgan as a distinctive breed. Like Canadians, Figure and his offspring, when bred to mares from other breeds, provided horses conforming to the best qualities of both. Figure was advertised at stud by Justin Morgan between 1792 and 1795, and stood for many years thereafter with different owners or renters.

Figure probably died at thirty-two, although his exact age is a matter of some historical confusion. At least one account has Figure's foaling as 1793, with the colt coming to

Justin Morgan in 1795. Whatever might have been Figure's age at death he and his progeny were kept very busy, and all that activity in the early years of the Morgan's shaping involved more than a few Canadian mares and stallions. Justin Morgan himself is recorded as having bred Figure to Canadian mares.

Just as the Canadian evolved into a unique breed and went on to sift into the bloodlines of other breeds, so did the Morgan. Morgan strains run through Standardbreds, English Hackneys, Tennessee Walking Horses, and American Saddlebreds. Except for the Hackneys, Canadian influence also appears in all of these breeds to varying degrees.

During the American Civil War, Union generals quickly realized the Morgan's positive attributes. The 1,030-member First Vermont Cavalry Regiment, famed as the Green Mountain Boys, to a man rode Morgans. Of the original 1,200 horses with the Regiment at the beginning of the war in 1861, 200 managed to survive to the surrender at Appomattox in 1865. Unlike other regiments, which had to obtain remounts wherever they could, the Green Mountain Boys were kept supplied with Morgan remounts from Vermont throughout the war. These horses served in seventy-five battles and skirmishes.

Other Union cavalry units that began with Morgans came from Maine, Michigan, Pennsylvania, and New York. There were two New Hampshire battalions in the First

Rhode Island Cavalry that listed their mounts as either Morgans or Canadians, but these two were the only units that made the distinction.

By the time the war began, indeed by the 1850s, Morgans were known as far west as California and at least as far south as Virginia. Only one Confederate unit is on record as entering the war with Morgans (Company H, Fourth Virginia Cavalry), but it is a Morgan that is among the most remembered of Confederate war horses. This was Little Sorrel, the favourite horse of General Stonewall Jackson. The general had acquired the horse as a gift for his wife, but soon discovered it was an ideal military mount. Both horse and rider became venerated heroes of the South.

The most famous horse of the war on the Union side was also a Morgan. This was a gelding named Rienzi, and by war's end he was a veteran of nineteen battles. From 1862 until the end of the war, Rienzi was General Phillip Sheridan's personal horse, and he may have saved Abraham Lincoln's presidency.

That came about in 1864, when morale was low on the Union side. The war had not been going well, and, since it was a presidential election year, any more losses on the battlefield might cost Lincoln victory at the polls. That October, just a month before the election, Sheridan learned that a major Confederate attack was under way at Cedar Creek, Virginia, and that his troops were being routed. The general, at Winchester, twelve miles from the battle, immediately gave Rienzi his rein. The horse had to gallop across broken countryside and down roads clogged with wounded troops, but his unwavering speed carried Sheridan to the front in time to rally the successful counterattack that proved to be pivotal to the war's outcome. A lesser horse might not have made it in time.

Lincoln was re-elected after the victory, and Sheridan eventually went on to become his Commanding General of the U.S. Army. Rienzi was renamed Winchester after the Cedar Creek battle and lived comfortably until 1878. When he died, the Army had him stuffed. He is still on display at the Smithsonian Institute's National Museum of American History.

Comanche, another famous American war horse, is believed to have been part Morgan. Comanche was wounded in battle three times before the day in 1876 when Seventh Cavalry Captain Myles Keogh rode him into the Little Big Horn River valley. Only one member of the Seventh Cavalry survived the battle there, that came to be known as Custer's Last Stand. That was Comanche, found wounded and wandering days later.

In a curious twist, it is possible that horses with Canadian bloodlines were used by both sides at the Little Big Horn. Many Sioux had fled west from Minnesota after their abortive 1862 uprising and the largest mass hanging in United States history (thirty-eight Sioux). It is known that they had "French horses," most certainly Canadians, for which they had traded. Northern Minnesota was populated by Chippewa, long-time friends of the French-Canadian and Métis traders, who might have had Canadians, and St. Paul, Minnesota was very much a French-Canadian settlement.

Indeed, until the Louisiana Purchase in 1803 the French had exercised nominal control over vast areas of the central Midwest, from Louisiana to Lake Superior. Place names such as St. Louis, Mobile, Biloxi, Terra Haute, and Des Moines date from that period. The Purchase included all of Missouri, Arkansas, Iowa, Oklahoma, Kansas, and Nebraska, and parts of Montana, Wyoming, North Dakota, South Dakota, New Mexico, and Colorado. Since Canadian horses were certainly exported to the French Caribbean colonies, they surely would also have found their way into these nominally French regions as well.

Genetic science may some day conclusively explain just how far the Canadians' influence spread.

Chapter 5 Canadians Cross the Continent

The British victory in the Seven Years War and the flight of Loyalists to Upper Canada after the American Revolution changed life for the Canadian horse. Arguably, it wasn't for the better.

The breed's isolation from other breeds was shattered. For a hundred years, the horse breed had developed with only negligible crossbreeding. To be sure, Quebecois had bred Canadians for selected qualities, but only from Canadian stock. Over many generations two distinct lines had been developed, one for work and the other, the "fancies," for racing, riding, and drawing carriages. Both lines, however, were true to the breed, unmistakably Canadian through and through. Crossbreeding did occur outside Quebec with Canadians that had been exported, however.

The influence of the Canadian spread in other ways besides intentional export. Notably in French-held Michigan and Illinois, French traders and settlers generally permitted their Canadians to range freely in herds when they were not required for tasks. In these natural herd environments older stallions would drive out the younger ones, which would form their own herds elsewhere. The number of exiles and runaways is unknown, but over decades there would have been many. They undoubtedly encountered and bred with other breeds such as Mustangs and Indian Cayuses. And before the Louisiana Purchase, Canadians were used as trade goods and as pack animals by French traders throughout the Midwestern United States. These, too, would likely have been exposed to other breeds.

But dramatic change arrived with the British and the Loyalists. They came with their own horses of various breeds and didn't hesitate to crossbreed them with Canadians, particularly when they realized the Canadians were better suited to the environment and the work. Perhaps even more important as an inducement to crossbreeding was the Canadian's prepotence; the breed's best qualities could be counted on to persist in the offspring. Unfortunately this practice eventually led to thinning of the Canadian blood line, or, as some put it, "the gradual mongrelizing of the breed."

Nevertheless, Canadians still managed to thrive. Many did so in the lumber camps, working to meet the huge demand for lumber to maintain the British merchant and navy fleets. Britain ruled the seas but it did so in wooden ships, many of which were built in Canadian shipyards from Canadian trees.

In Quebec and the Maritimes shipbuilding became a major industry. Shipyards stretched for twenty kilometres along both banks of the Miramichi River. Shipyards and timber storage facilities blanketed the St. Lawrence River's northern shoreline between Lévis and Lauzon. At least one shipyard employed a thousand workers, and all the shipyards used many horses.

Horses also served in the vast forest complexes that supplied the yards with timber. Oxen had been used at first, but it was soon found that Canadians could haul more wood faster than oxen, they were good for other work that oxen could not do, and they were easier and cheaper to maintain.

Typically, work in the forest began in the fall with the first snow. Logging crews, often numbering 300 men and 100 or more horses, would cut roads into the bush and build a winter camp. When the waterways froze over, the real work began. Horses hauled cut logs from the bush to the road, where the logs were trimmed and piled on sleighs. The road downhill to the frozen waterway would be kept coated in ice, so the heavy sleighs would slip relatively easily—sometimes too easily—down to the frozen waterway where the logs could be offloaded from the sleighs and piled, waiting for the spring thaw that would carry them downstream to the lumber yards and the shipbuilders. At the end of each day's work, horses would haul great water wagons along the icy downhill road, renewing the ice coating like an early-day rink resurfacer, making the road clean and ready for tomorrow.

The loads could be huge. Sometimes they were three or four times the height of a horse and the same distance wide. Two-horse teams of the powerful little Canadians would be used for the heaviest loads, but sometimes even at that the dead weight was too much for the horses to get moving on the icy surface. For those loads the drivers would have the horses first pull to one side, then to the other side, until the load broke free and started moving on the downhill run.

Now there was another problem. The road's surface was slick enough that the horses could keep the loads moving, but if the downhill angle were steep the laden sleighs might pick up so much speed they would overrun the horses and hurtle off the road into the bush, scattering the load, wrecking the sleigh, and probably killing the horses.

While horses were generally considered expendable, the sleighs were not. Nor were the man-hours that would be required to reload the logs onto another sleigh. To prevent such runaway loads—luckily for the horses—men known as "groundhogs" walked beside the sleigh with buckets of sand, ready to throw sand under the runners if the sleigh started to speed out of control. The sand acted as an effective brake.

Canadian lumber was in demand for more than shipbuilding. By the 1830s, as industrialization rose, lumber exports to Britain and the United States soared. Small wood products such as barrel staves, shingles, and box shooks (slices of wood ready to be used in making boxes) were exported in shipload quantities. The demand for railroad ties in both countries, especially the United States, burgeoned. From 1848 to World War I, exports of wood and wood products averaged 600,000 tons annually—to Britain alone!

As the forests of timber close to the ports were depleted, the loggers moved further inland, taking the Canadians with them. Then, with land laid bare, farming took hold in some regions. The southwestern townships of Quebec and the eastern counties of Ontario, for example, became fertile agricultural land that was second in quality only to parts of the Prairies. From forest to field, just as it had done in the early habitant settlements, the Canadian horse again made an easy, seamless transition.

Loyalist settlers in Upper Canada discovered the Canadians' virtues before the turn of the nineteenth century, and the breed became as indispensable to the Loyalists as it had been for the habitants. And Upper Canadians were also aware of the breed's remarkable prepotence. Crossbreeding was not only inevitable as they sought to develop a better horse, but commonplace. Unfortunately, discrimination was not always used.

The Canadians' contributions to Upper Canada's development were certainly significant, but so much crossbreeding was devastating to the breed's integrity. To make it worse, the Upper Canadians were not alone. Except for a hiatus during the War of 1812, demand for the horse was also high in the United States, and the same effects resulted there.

Horse prices in the United States had been driven up enough to provide an excellent profit for American traders willing to come up to Quebec ("Lower Canada") and buy Canadians. As many as 1,000 horses a week were sold at the Montreal horse market for shipment to the United States and the West Indies. The days when Benedict Arnold could fill a couple of wagons with cheese, utensils, textiles, and other merchandise and trade for a small herd of fine Canadians were gone, though. Now demand was so competitive that American traders sent agents into the townships to negotiate directly with owners, and several poor crop years had left many farmers in dire circumstances. Their horses were all they had left to sell, and many farmers were willing to accept low prices. The American trader would often throw a poor-quality horse into the deal, so that the farmer would have at least something to replace his Canadians, but those horses crossbred with such Canadians as remained, and crossbreeding thus became common in Lower Canada. As if that weren't enough, American traders favoured Canadian stallions, which could service common mares in the south. Canadian stallion stock rapidly dwindled, particularly from the 1830s to the 1850s.

The breeding value of Canadian stallions was emphasized in an American report in 1857:

> *A black stallion imported from Canada, a few years since, by Mr. John Legg, of Skaneateles, New York, has got several hundred colts, which, when broken, have averaged about one hundred dollars a piece in value; a sum considerably above the average prices of horses in the country. They are almost invariably fair roadsters, and excellent farm horses. This cross is more and more finding favour among farmers.*

To the north, alarm bells began ringing about the same time. Veterinarians in Lower Canada began to realize that the quality of the horses they saw was steadily but surely deteriorating because of the interbreeding with cheap American stallions. The American traders, who knew what was happening long before anyone else, stopped buying stallions in Quebec.

The original Canadian breed may have seemed threatened with extinction, but horses carrying its dominating bloodlines persisted in more isolated parts of Lower Canada. The Canadians were not about to fade away. After all, their ancestors had been the country's original equine survivalists. Moreover, by then Canadians were making their influence felt in other parts of North America.

Before rail travel, immigrants going west to settle the prairies did so in wagons pulled by oxen or horses, usually horses. Many of these horses, purchased in Upper Canada or in the former French holdings from the Lakehead westward, carried Canadian genes. By the time settlers from the British Isles and Upper Canada arrived to take up land grants, French-Canadian settlements dotted the landscape from Manitoba to Alberta, and these earlier settlers already had "French horses," likely brought into the region as wagon and pack animals to facilitate trade.

As they worked their prairie land grants, these settlers—like others before them—found that horses could outperform oxen in almost every task, provided many other advantages, and were a lot cheaper. The Canadians had just one more mountain to climb before they could properly be said to be the whole nation's horse: the Rockies.

The Cariboo gold rush of 1861 provided the opportunity. While most people seeking their fortune in the Cariboo chose to travel by ship to the west coast, then by various

A Canadian stallion from West Gimlet Farms braving the elements on a pack trip to the Yukon.

means up the Cariboo Trail, one large party from Upper Canada decided in 1862 to go cross-country to the gold field. They became known in Canadian history as the Overlanders.

Using horses and oxen acquired in Upper Canada, the Overlanders party reached present-day Edmonton without difficulty. Now they had to cross the mountains to penetrate

British Columbia's interior. They selected the Yellowhead Pass, a route mapped by David Thompson many years earlier but never used. The going was slow and treacherous. Trails had to be cut for the wagons and oxen. Roundabout routes had to be found because the oxen could not master the mountainous terrain. The horses, on the other hand, had no problem with it.

The Overlanders had assumed that they could easily live off the land. They were familiar with Upper Canada, back east, at that time still teeming with deer, moose, bears, and game birds. But mountains provide scarcer fare. Unpredictable, fierce weather in the highlands caused long delays. As supplies ran low and starvation threatened, the party decided to split in two, one to forge ahead and the other to follow.

Misfortune followed misfortune as the Overlanders continued toward their Eldorado. Four died, swept away in a rapids. But, ragged and starving though they were, the rest were getting close.

Then they encountered an impasse. They would have to complete the journey on water; the remaining livestock, about 100 horses and oxen, would have to be abandoned. The Overlanders slaughtered the oxen for meat and turned the horses loose in the wilderness (which, very likely, didn't trouble the horses in the slightest).

Today, nearly 150 years later, on a high plateau in the

Chilcotin region known as the Brittany Triangle, west of where those horses were abandoned, lives the only wild horse herd in British Columbia. Although the horses are considered by many to be mustangs, First Nations oral history in the area holds that the horses did not appear there until the gold rush days, suggesting that these animals, or at least some of them, may be descended from the Overlanders' horses.

The mustang theory suggests descent from runaways that escaped from the herds of the Okanagan and Nez Perce tribes to the south. The probability that Canadian blood ran through the Overlanders' horses is strong, though, and Canadian DNA has been identified in northern mustangs and other horses used by the First Nations. It is also possible that some of the original Brittany Triangle horses were runaways—horses brought to the area by gold prospectors (as pack animals) or by freight wagon and stagecoach operators. Most likely, all three sources have been involved.

Unfortunately, history will have to wait for definitive DNA testing of the Chilcotin herd to confirm whether Canadians did indeed make it across continental Canada.

Chapter 6
Canada's War Horse

Canada did not become a nation simply by flooding the country with settlers and their Canadian horses. To secure the land also required the use of military and paramilitary force.

Until the end of the nineteenth century, horses were as essential to the military as motorized vehicles are today. In Canada, that usually meant Canadians. The distinctive Canadian was ridden into battle during the Seven Years War, the American Revolution, the War of 1812–14, and the rebellions of 1837 in Upper and Lower Canada.

Between 1866 and 1871, Canadian horses were once more pressed into service to defend our borders against invaders. The threat came from Irish-Americans known as

"Montcalm Leading his Troops at the Plains of Abraham" by Charles William Jeffreys (1869–1951).

Fenians. The Fenians' long-term objective was to free Ireland from British rule, not at the bargaining tables but on the battlefields, and the battlefields they chose were along the Canadian border from the St. Lawrence River to Manitoba.

Their leadership believed that a Fenian takeover of Canada would divert British attention from Ireland, inspire Irish patriots in the homeland, and provide a springboard to eventually free Ireland.

They also believed that Irish-Canadians, of whom there were a considerable number, would rally to their cause once they achieved a foothold in Canada. North of the border, along the St. Lawrence and Lakes Ontario and Erie, citizens and the soon-to-be Canadian government saw the Fenians as a clear and present danger.

Many Fenian recruits and their officers were seasoned veterans of the American Civil War. Initially they were well-financed, thanks to contributions from Irish-American sympathizers. And, in the beginning, the American government turned a blind eye while the Fenians stockpiled arms and other military supplies along the border, clearly in violation of the U.S. Neutrality Act.

At the time, Canada must have appeared to be a soft target. Since the Crimean War of the mid-1850s, needing the troops elsewhere, Britain had been reducing its military garrisons in North America. Neither Upper nor Lower Canada had a standing army to replace them, and the militias, first formed in 1855, though over-subscribed by volunteers, trained only a few days each year.

Canada was not a soft target. Canadian authorities had excellent intelligence regarding Fenian plans and logistics at all times, because the man in charge of supply procurement for the Fenians, Henri Le Caron, was a spy in the pay of the Canadians and the British.

In the belief that their forces would face a poorly equipped, disorganized, untrained resistance that would melt away back to the farms and towns as soon as they crossed the border, the Fenians were so confident that when their cash ran short they made arrangements with their troops and the wagon drovers hauling supplies to give them unrestrained right to looting in the eventual "conquered land" as payment for their services.

The Fenians were also mistaken in thinking that Irish-Canadians north of the border would rally to the Fenian cause. The opposite occurred. Half a dozen times the Fenians mounted raids, committing their troops in the hundreds, before their final, minor foray into Manitoba in 1871. In the east, each time they attempted a raid they were quickly repulsed, suffering many more casualties than the country's defenders. The abortive raid in Manitoba found them capturing Pembina, only to be arrested by the U.S. Army—fortunately for the Fenians, because Manitoba had just become a proud province of Canada and several hundred angry, fiercely loyal Canadian volunteers were en route to do worse to them.

Mobility was critical to the Canadians' success, and horses were the key. Unless volunteers were within a mile or two of a probable raid, they piled into horse-drawn wagons and rode to the site, arriving quickly and well-rested. Other volunteers, and most officers, brought their own horses. Local farmers were quick to hitch their teams to their wagons for troops and supplies. Travel time could be reduced from more than a day to a few hours, giving troops ample time to assemble where a raid was expected, sort themselves out, and prepare their defences. The light draft Canadians were ideal for these purposes, and they were plentiful in the regions where the Fenians attacked.

Not every nineteenth-century domestic military operation that required horses worked out so well, though; at least, not for the troops.

By 1874 sovereignty was an issue in the North-West Territories, which then comprised parts of present-day Saskatchewan, Alberta, British Columbia, the Yukon, and Nunavut. The borders with the United States were still disputed and Americans freely hunted and traded on the Canadian side. Not only did the Canadian government feel compelled to demonstrate its sovereignty, it also sought to bring law and order to the region.

The pervasiveness of the illegal trade in whiskey with Natives in the Territory and an 1873 incident in Canada's Cypress Hills—American wolf hunters indiscriminately killed a number of Assiniboines—spurred the government to form the North West Mounted Police.

The first 150 members were recruited and underwent training in Ottawa. The training was elementary. Some recruits had never before ridden a horse.

From Ottawa they travelled by train and boat to the Lakehead. From there they travelled on horseback to Winnipeg. This latter phase was the actual beginning of a journey that became known as the North West Mounted Police's Great Trek West.

The terrain through which they rode was as rough and treacherous as any Canada has to offer. There were fast-moving rivers, swamps, thick bush, steep rocky hills, and, of course, clouds of mosquitoes and blackflies. The weather ranged from hot and stiflingly humid to frigid, and there were torrential rainstorms.

It would probably be wrong to assume that all of their horses were Canadians, but many either were or, at least, carried a strong Canadian bloodline. The area where the first horses would have been purchased was well-known for its Canadians. The Mounties needed horses that were even-tempered enough to tolerate beginner riders, yet strong enough for the arduous tasks to come. That Canadians could also draw supply wagons and function as pack animals were other incentives to select them. Clearly, as well, anyone familiar with U.S. Civil War records would know the Canadians' value under fire.

More breed variety may have been added when two

more contingents of recruits joined the force, mostly from western Canada, where many of the horses were still "French horses."

From Winnipeg, accompanied by a long wagon train, the Mounties set off to establish a policing presence on the Prairies. In many respects this part of the trek was as arduous as that from the Lakehead. There were no endless fields of golden grain swaying in the breeze, nor were there roads. The tracks were rough and narrow. Though the swamps that the Mounties had crossed in northern Ontario were replaced by briny, often stagnant alkali sloughs, insects were as bad as they had been in the Ontario bush. If there was an advantage in the flatlands, it was that storms could be seen coming from miles away. Nevertheless, the Mounties successfully established posts along the southern part of the Prairies.

The Mounties were a paramilitary rather than a military unit, a police force structured along military lines. Horses remained mainstays for their work in western Canada until World War I. Perhaps taking a page from their book, a lesson learned, so to speak, many urban police forces today still maintain an operational—as opposed to a ceremonial—mounted unit. Four of the seven-horse Calgary Police unit are Canadians and, to a horse, Montreal's mounted unit are all Canadians.

During the late nineteenth century, horses would twice again be called on to support domestic military actions. The first was the 1885 Riel Rebellion in Saskatchewan.

From the government's point of view, the perceived threat had three elements: the Métis; a numerous Cree population; and sympathizers in Montana, notably those with an eye toward annexing the Canadian prairies to the United States. As quickly as possible, the government assembled, equipped, and dispatched a volunteer military force to quell the rebellion.

The presence of the new continental railroad in Saskatchewan enabled the soldiers to arrive quickly, but the march north from the railway to the rebellious area was made difficult by the beginning of spring thaw. The troops were beset by subzero temperatures, blizzards, and freezing rain. Streams were ice-choked torrents, and muskeg, frozen over at night, became bottomless bog when daytime temperatures rose. Adding to the difficulties, the 8,000-strong military force was bringing horse-drawn light artillery.

As was customary, officers were on horseback and the infantry had to march on foot. The troops showed great courage and perseverance, but it was likely the horses—equally valiant—who made progress possible.

Schooled in static warfare tactics in the European tradition, the soldiers found that the Métis and Cree were more fluid. They no more marched into battle in carefully arranged lines than the Iroquois had centuries before. Eventually, though, the army finally managed to besiege the main body of Métis at Batoche. Superior numbers, artillery, and a Gatling gun won the day. The Cree militants were eventually cornered and defeated as well. The message across the West was clear: Canada would defend its territory.

But there were those who didn't quite get it. In 1898 the need to defend the Canadian border arose again, this time because of the Klondike gold rush and a simmering Canada-U.S. dispute over the location of the Alaska–British Columbia border along the Alaskan Panhandle.

As during the earlier Cariboo gold rush and on other occasions, Americans tended to claim the protection of their own government. In the Cariboo the British Royal Engineers had exercised unequivocal sovereignty, but elsewhere the British had been forced to cede a significant part of present-day Oregon when they had been unable to demonstrate their authority. Now thousands of Americans were descending on the Klondike.

In May 1898 the Canadian government sent a contingent of 203 volunteer troops to the Yukon to support the thinly-spread North West Mounted Police. Known as the Yukon Field Force, these troops were drawn from the Royal Canadian Regiment and the Royal Canadian Dragoons, the latter a cavalry unit. Every hope was that a show of arms would be enough to ensure order. Indeed, the Force was equipped with some of the most modern arms available, including two Maxim guns, the first automatic machine guns.

Part of their journey required a 320-kilometre march from Telegraph Creek to Fort Selkirk, rain and mosquitoes all the way, and, for fifty of the troops, an additional march to Dawson Creek, where they established a second garrison. From the diary of Trooper Edward Lester:

> *The way lay along the margin of a chain of lakes, sometimes through the depths of a forest, now running through a gloomy gorge with beetling crags overhead, now crossing a mountain torrent, now winding over a shaking bog, over a corduroy road a slip from which meant a plunge to the knees in black peaty slime.*

Between the Mounties' controlling access to the gold field and the two garrisons "on guard," the gold rush ran its course in relative peace and good order. The last members of the Yukon Field Force left the north in the summer of 1900.

The Field Force very probably had horses with Canadian blood, because by then the Canadians' qualities had made them the military's horse of choice for light draft duties no matter what the task. Soon the Canadians would be tested on battlefields thousands of miles away.

Chapter 7
South of the Border

By the mid-1850s the Canadian horse had met or exceeded every demand placed on it by the country's early settlers. From fewer than a hundred, the breed had multiplied to 150,000. Through crossbreeding, also known as outbreeding, they had already influenced the characteristics of hundreds of thousands of other North American domestic horses.

The Canadians' strength, stamina, and remarkable prepotence ensured their renown, not just at home but south of the border as well. In the United States, farmers and merchants who owned Canadians were typically delighted with the breed's ability to work hard yet almost never show fatigue.

Still, Canadians were much more than just common work horses. In the early nineteenth century, the Canadians' racing prowess stunned fans of the sport all the way to New Orleans. The most famous of the Canadian pacers was a black stallion variously known as Pacing Pilot, Old Pilot, Canadian Pilot, and, naturally, just Pilot. Old Pilot was foaled in 1823 to Quebecker Louis Dansereau, then sold at the Montreal horse market six years later. Two years after that, Old Pilot turned up in New Orleans.

The stallion's forte as a racing pacer (a pacer moves both feet on the same side in unison) had been identified by then. In one New Orleans race he clocked a mile at 2 minutes 26 seconds; this during a period when 2:30 was considered an almost certain winning time. (After refinements to equipment, tracks, training, and veterinary science, and selective purpose-breeding, the standard for the mile is now two minutes or less.) Old Pilot didn't linger in New Orleans. No other owners were willing to put their horses up against him. He was taken to Kentucky, where he was advertised at stud.

When Old Pilot was twenty-one years old he sired a foal named Pilot Jr. Until Jr., most of Old Pilot's foals had been pacers. Jr. was an exception. He was a natural trotter (a trotter moves each front foot on one side in unison with the back foot on the other side) and most of his offspring would also be trotters. Jr. was also the horse that would make the Pilot lineage famous.

Rather than gaining fame from the stallions he sired, as was usual, Jr. made his mark through his daughters. Two were especially notable: Midnight and Miss Russell. Among the foals eventually born to Midnight, six trotted consistently at 2:26 and one of these, Jay-Eye-See, was the first horse to set a time of 2:10. Another granddaughter, Maud S., foaled by the mare Miss Russell, was the first trotter to break the 2:10 mark, an astonishing speed for that era. The Pilot line would become a prominent part of the foundation stock for Standardbred horses, currently one of the most numerous breeds in the world.

The nineteenth century should have been exciting, fruitful times for the Canadian breed. Their value to the development of Canada—as settlers pushed westward and loggers opened the forests—was unsurpassed by that of any other breed. They had also become important to Canada's young military. Unfortunately, their success was to bring their very existence into question by the end of the century.

Since the first settlements on the continent, the population of the United States had always been higher than that of Canada. During the nineteenth century it mushroomed, not just in the cities but westward across former French, Spanish, and Native American territories all the way to the Pacific Ocean. Many immigrants reached American shores by ship, but once their feet hit dry ground they needed horses to move inland. The surge of westward settlement created such a high demand for horses that satisfying it became a spark that started the 1846–48 Mexican War.

Travelling by stagecoach near the Clearwater River in Alberta with Canadians from West Gimlet Farms.

The matter of horses being stolen from Mexican territory and sold in the U.S.—a cause of the war—may seem to have little to do with the Canadian breed. But, in fact, the influx of Spanish horses from Mexico may have been quite important to the Canadians' influence on the development of other breeds in the Midwestern plains.

During the years preceding the war, enterprising horse wranglers had made forays into Texas and south of the Rio Grande into Mexico itself to round up horses, despite Mexican protests that the horses were their property. These herds, some of which numbered as many as 1,000, were driven to St. Joseph, Missouri, which was the main jumping-off point for settlers heading west and therefore, at the time, perhaps the largest horse market in North America.

Although this demand and the subsequent war would have no direct effect on Canadian stock in Canada, the significant exposure of the "French horses" still in America's former French territory to the new, predominately Spanish stock would, on one hand, dilute the Canadian blood line in the U.S. but, on the other, enhance the breeds of horses in the plains region. Breed lines in the United States would become extremely blurred, practically their only continuity among smaller, lighter horses being attributable to the prepotence of the "French horses."

But the Canadian breed's distinctiveness in the "old Canadian"—the horse that had first brought fame to the breed—was under siege. The siege was subtle, disguised by the breed's apparent success in the marketplace. Except to a handful of breeders and experts in Canada, the siege was invisible. Then came the American Civil War and, following closely, the Indian Wars.

When the Civil War started in 1861, there were estimated to be 5.1 million horses in the United States, plus an additional 800,000 in the Kentucky and Missouri territories. By the time the war ended in 1865, the U.S. horse population had been reduced by twenty per cent. One might have assumed that the Americans had enough horses of their own for both sides to carry out their war. This was not the case.

Only a small percentage of America's horses were suitable for military use, and many of these were far away from the principal war zones.

Just as wars seem to require the youngest and strongest citizens, these wars needed specific types of horses. For example, for cavalry purposes the Union armies demanded mares and geldings four to five years old, and, for the artillery, mares and geldings six years or older. Over the war's duration the Union side would field 272 cavalry regiments and the Confederates 137. While most of these were chronically undermanned, all required horses to ride into action, plus remounts for replacement purposes.

Early in the war the Union armies favoured using Morgan horses, partly because they were plentiful and readily available. This was especially so for the Army of the Potomac. However, with an average of 500 horses a week being lost (more to disease, exhaustion, and malnutrition than to battle), Union eyes turned to Canada.

The north-south export horse trade was already well-established. With the Union Army paying $150 each for horses already trained to saddle or wagon, there was good profit to be made in selling Canadians to the Union Army. As well, the Army sent its own purchasing agents to Quebec and eastern Ontario to deal directly with breeders and wholesalers. By the end of the war an estimated 30,000 Canadians had been shipped to the Union. Equally desperate for horses, operating in a more clandestine fashion because of shipping blockades, the Confederates also purchased Canadians in indeterminate numbers. Indeed, the South became so desperate for pack animals that at one time they imported a number of camels for service, along with an Algerian camel driver. That did not work out well, but some Canadian horses did get through and saw action on the Confederate side. Overall, twenty per cent or more of available Canadian stock went south, never to return.

Horses were indispensable, but individual horses were disposable.

Excerpts from an 1863 letter written by Charles Francis Adams, an officer of the 17th Pennsylvania Volunteer Cavalry, Company E, graphically describes the conditions the horses endured:

> *I have but one rule, a horse must go on until he can't be spurred further...imagine a horse with his withers swollen to three times the natural size, and with a volcanic, running sore pouring matter down each side, and you have a case with which every cavalry officer is daily called upon to deal, and you imagine a horse which*

> *has still to be ridden until he lays down in sheer suffering under the saddle...the air of Virginia is literally burdened today by the stench of dead horses, federal and confederate. You pass them on every road and find them in every field.*

The fate of the horses used by artillery units was no better. Although mules were generally used to move artillery and to pack ammunition from place to place, they were useless in actual fighting. Mules would panic under fire, even endangering their handlers. Therefore, to move the artillery close enough to engage the enemy, horses were hitched to the limbers.

These could not be just any horses and, especially on the Union side (and unfortunately for the Canadians), it was Canadians who were especially suited for the task. Sure-footed over broken ground, strong, and hardly ever given to panic, they would have attracted immediate attention during the training undergone by every horse destined for Union army artillery service. Because the ideal horse would lie down in the heat of battle, to graduate horses had to pass a test, hauling artillery while under fire from Gatling guns and rifles. At first the live fire would be directed over their heads. Then it would be lowered to a lethal level. If the horse laid down and stayed down, it graduated. If it didn't...well, it failed. Truly, this was an unforgiving school of hard knocks.

Graduation brought no laurels. As soon as they were taken into action the horses became high-value targets to the enemy. To kill or disable artillery horses immobilized the guns, either keeping them out of action or, better, leaving them vulnerable to capture. Captured guns were especially valuable to the Confederates, because they usually had far less firepower of their own than the Union side did.

As the war dragged on, both sides stole the other's horses for remounts. The Union's specifications for qualified horses were thrown out the window. Now any horse would do. The same had held for the Confederates for some time. During the Gettysburg campaigns, for example, Confederate Jeb Stuart's cavalry conducted a raid in Pennsylvania that commandeered 1,000 unbroken horses from local farmers and townspeople. That raid was solely about obtaining horses—a measure of their importance in the conflict.

Many U.S. Army horses, including Canadians, survived the Civil War, but for some good fortune was short-lived. Almost immediately after the smoke cleared the U.S. Cavalry turned its considerable force against Native Americans in the Midwest from Texas to the Canadian border. Like the Morgans, any Canadians left in the Army were moved west for the Indian Wars that cleared the way for European-American settlement all way to the Pacific.

In 1874–75 the North West Mounted Police wanted

to prosecute white Americans for murdering Natives on Canadian soil during the Cypress Hills Massacre. The American media wasted no time in expressing disgust at such a notion. Then, as now, the idea that a foreign country would dare prosecute Americans for anything was viewed as a gross insult to the United States.

Such an event not only indicates the temper of the times in Washington, where the Monroe Doctrine had taken firm hold and eventually would be used to justify aggressive action globally, but is a strong indicator of attitudes in the Midwest at the time. The government's success in the Indian Wars was a foregone conclusion. The government had the arms, manpower, and horses, and the settlers had a tacit licence to kill. Nevertheless, not all of the Natives went quietly.

While few "old Canadians" would have been involved in action during these years, many horses on both sides would have carried "old Canadian" genes. The same has been suggested for the horses of the legendary Pony Express and the Wells Fargo stage lines in the west.

The Pony Express operated for nineteen months before the transcontinental telegraph effectively put it out of business. The company delivered mail across 2,000 miles between St. Joseph, Missouri, and Sacramento, California, from April 1860 to October 1861. Most of the horses were bought in St. Joseph, Sacramento, and Salt Lake, and Canadians are known to have been in California from at least the time of the gold rush in 1849, when a herd of 150 was transported there. Doubtless, too, there would have been Canadians at formerly-French St. Joseph. For the Pony Express *not* to have used Canadians would be unlikely, given their known qualities of remarkable stamina and easy keeping.

The legendary Wells Fargo stagecoach line, the largest in the world during its heyday, began in 1852. Its main purpose was to provide regular mail service between St. Louis and San Francisco. The company's famous Concord stagecoaches, drawn by six-horse teams, would have used many more horses than the Pony Express. For sake of speed and stamina, these would have been light draft horses—mustangs, Morgans, Standardbreds, and, of course, Canadians when available. Canadians had already proven themselves on stage lines in the northeastern United States, especially when bred with slightly heavier horses. Wells Fargo purchasing agents would have sought horses with the same qualities, and "French horses" were definitely available in the Midwest.

While the number of Canadians was somewhat reduced during the years prior to the Civil War, the war itself had a devastating impact. Stallions were exported from Canada in large numbers, and many were gelded. So, too, were thousands of mares exported, at an age when they would otherwise have begun to produce foals. Generations of future Canadians were wiped out, when the breed's present numbers were already dwindling. That its genes were now being carried in other breeds throughout North America was small consolation.

Chapter 8
In Defence of Empire

Although Canada has never unilaterally declared war on another nation, its mutual defence agreements with other countries have drawn it into military conflicts.

The first of these "official" involvements was the 1899–1902 Boer War or, as it is sometimes known, the South African War. This is not to say that Canadians had not had prior involvements. Canadian volunteers had joined the British Army to fight in the 1846–48 Crimean War, and Canada did provide military supplies to other countries, notably the horses sold south during the U.S. Civil War that resulted in the sudden, dramatic reduction in the Canadian breed population.

By 1899, when the Boer War started, breeders of Canadians were well aware that the "old Canadians" were nearly gone, and that even the number of horses that retained most of the old Canadians' finest qualities was diminishing. Fortunately, this helped reduce the number sold when the military came calling. It helped, too, that some Quebeckers were reluctant to support British military ventures.

But perhaps the most compelling deterrent to selling Canadians to the military was the concern that the breed was becoming scarce. A registration program was by then in place for the breed, too, and registered horses commanded a higher price than the military was willing to pay.

In English Canada, though, enthusiasm for the British Empire's causes was high, mostly fuelled by a substantial population of first- and second-generation British immigrants. Given that base, 7,000 volunteers went off to fight for the Empire in South Africa. The volunteers fought in their own units with their own field officers but did so under overall British strategic command. All of these volunteers relied directly or indirectly on horses, the first of which accompanied them from Canada.

Embarking from eastern Canada, mainly from Quebec City and Montreal, the troops travelled on the same ships as the horses. Despite many Quebeckers' reluctance to sell their Canadians, some had found the British pound irresistible, as had many other owners, particularly from eastern Ontario, so Canadians went, too.

For military purposes Canadians and their close relatives were the most sought after, closely followed by Morgans, which were still plentiful in the New England states. As had occurred during the Civil War, the British wanted four- and five-year-old mares and geldings for its cavalry and mounted infantry, and six-year-olds and up as pack animals and artillery haulers; once again, these were horses entering what should have been the years of their greatest productivity.

Only a small percentage of the Boer War horses came from Canada. Britain acquired a hundred thousand horses in the United States, and many more in Ireland, Argentina, Australia, and New Zealand. On that grand scale of British purchases, the Canadians were few; but as a percentage of the shrinking pool of Canadians available, though, they were a major sacrifice of the breed...and sacrificed they were.

British war planners estimated that at least twenty per cent of horses would die in transit, before ever reaching South Africa. As for the survivors, their remaining life span was estimated to average six weeks.

The short life span was only in a small part attributable to the ferocity of the battles. Once in South Africa the horses were given no opportunity to rest or become acclimated to the weather or terrain before going directly to the front. Most of the troops were inexperienced horsemen with little, if any, knowledge of how to take care of a horse.

This was not of much help to the cause, for, as Canadian Lieutenant General Sir A. C. MacDonell put it: "No shoe, no foot; no foot, no horse; no horse, no transport; no transport, no battalion."

Once in the field, horses were often overloaded with a rider, his equipment, and supplies—the saddle alone weighed fifty pounds. Yet day after day the horses were ridden for long stretches without rest. On one occasion, a column on the move had 500 horses die of exhaustion—in a single day. On another, a British mounted division rode their horses to death in an operation that proved to be unnecessary. Only 1,500 of that division's 5,000 horses survived, and it was months before the unit returned to full strength.

The horses were rarely treated with sensitivity. When the Boers laid siege to Kimberley, British horses inside the town even lost their military status. They were deemed part of the available food supply and became, at the stroke of a bean-counter's pencil, just eighty-two tons of horsemeat. With additional accounting adjustments their feed also became part of the human food supply. On the books, directly and indirectly, the horses became enough food to last for two months.

The British who were besieged at Mafeking for 219 days were even more resourceful. Horseshoes were melted down to be moulded into ammunition. Manes and tails were shorn to use as mattress stuffing. The meat was used for steaks and sausage. Bones became a reportedly excellent base for a soup. The skin, head, and feet were boiled and then ground. The resulting mash would gel when cooled, rather like head cheese, and was known as brawn. One (dis)mounted trooper is on record as declaring a horse steak as tasty as beef.

At the best of times British food rations for troops were meagre and unpalatable. As Jack Heron of the Royal Canadian Regiment put it, "We don't get very much issued to us, in fact if we lived on Government rations we would starve in about a week but we manage to make up by commandeering from the Boers." Another way the soldiers "made up" was to eat the grain that was supposed to be fed to the horses.

Exhaustion and malnutrition—both were deadlier for horses than bullets. Disease was also a major cause of horse fatalities. Typically, horses died from strangles, glanders, flu accompanied by pink eye, and viral strains as alien to horses from the Western Hemisphere as smallpox had been to Natives in North America. Only the Canadians seemed to have resistance to the diseases specific to Africa, an asset that may have singled them out for a little more care than was given other breeds. This and the Canadians' inherent resilience probably helped them beat the odds and survive longer than six weeks.

Not all of the Canadian volunteers in the Boer War were inexperienced horsemen. One regiment, Lord Strathcona's Horse, was primarily made up of former and serving North

Trooper, Lord Strathcona's Horse, World War I.

West Mounted Police and cowboys from the Prairies. Because the regiment was privately financed by Lord Strathcona, special permission of the Canadian government was required. The Regiment's members acquitted themselves so well in

South Africa, where the British nicknamed them "The Headhunters," that at the beginning of World War I the "Strathies" were re-formed as a regular regiment in the Canadian Army.

Although there is no record of the breeds of horses the regiment took to South Africa, presumably they would have selected the best available, which would have led them to Canadians and their cousins, the Morgans. Unfortunately, of 599 horses that left Canada with the unit on March 17, 1900, 127 died en route or on the dock shortly after landing.

Luckily, the horses that did survive the trip had a month to rest and get used to the climate and terrain before they were pressed into action. From then, though, over the year that the regiment was in South Africa, original horses slowly disappeared and were replaced with horses from the British remount pool.

The Strathconas were constantly on the move. Primarily used as scouts for the main forces, they were the point of the spear and often had unsupported first contact with Boer fighters, who many times outnumbered them.

On the fifth of July, 1900, in its second month of action, a Strathcona patrol was ambushed by Boers. A former Mountie, Sergeant A. H. L. Richardson, saw a corporal shot from his saddle and fall wounded to the ground. Richardson turned his horse and, under heavy fire from the Boer snipers, galloped back to the corporal, dismounted, threw him over his saddle, and rushed back to rejoin his troops. Apart from some bullet holes in his uniform, Richardson was unscathed. His horse, wounded several times, had managed to bring back both men to safety, only to die later. Richardson was awarded the Victoria Cross, the first to be awarded a Canadian in the war.

Four months later, in November, horses once again came through for the Canadians, this time for the Royal Canadian Dragoons. Providing rearguard cover for a slow British infantry and artillery column, the Dragoons withstood repeated Boer assaults through the day, often counterattacking the determined Boers to hold them with close-quarter fighting. As a result of their actions that day—saving the artillery from being captured and turned against them, and preventing the capture of the foot soldiers—three Dragoons, Lieutenants Hampden Cockburn and Richard Turner and Sergeant Edward Holland, natives of Toronto, Quebec City, and Ottawa respectively, were awarded Victoria Crosses. The fate of the horses they used that day is unrecorded.

Eventually, the Boers were overwhelmed by the sheer number of British troops hurled against them, and the waste laid to their countryside. During the latter part of the war, the Boers resorted to very effective guerrilla tactics, supported by local farmers and villagers. The British response was to burn crops and buildings and slaughter livestock, starving the guerrillas into submission. Civilians—men, women, and children—were forced into overcrowded, disease-ridden internment camps. Curiously, Americans were using the same tactic at the same time, to stifle resistance in the Philippines during the Spanish-American War.

The Boer War was not the last in which Canadian horses would be used outside the North American continent, though. That dubious distinction goes to World War I.

European armies still relied on the use of horses then. A 1907 British cavalry training manual expressed the "heroic" image long nurtured for cavalry units: "It must be accepted in principle that the rifle, effective as it is, cannot replace the effect produced by the speed of the horse, the magnetism of the charge, and the terror of cold steel."

Tactically, the mobility of mounted troops served well in the ever-shifting fluid actions of the Boer War, but there was very little "magnetism of the charge." What evolved instead were units of mounted infantry, soldiers who would ride to an action and then dismount to fight.

World War I would provide the last hurrah for the use of cavalry in warfare. The "terror of cold steel" was replaced by the incessant chatter of machine guns and their torrent of hot steel. The open ground needed for gallant, sweeping cavalry charges was replaced by an impassable sea of mud laced with trenches and mines. One account from Passchendaele describes the plight of horses trying to supply ammunition: "many horses, on the short stretch…from the road to the battery, 80 yards of ground, sank down out of sight, the driver just keeping the head up until assistance arrived." When medics could not evacuate the wounded from the front lines because of the mud, horses were used to haul them out on sledges. The horse-drawn wagons were never empty. The horses would haul in food and ammunition, then haul out wounded soldiers, almost always under fire. Any romanticism the clash of great armies may have held for poets and armchair generals was shown to be a lie by the daily horrors on the front, for horses and men alike.

Canadian soldiers, particularly Strathcona's Horse, are remembered for what was among the last cavalry charges of World War I and one of the last in history. It took place in France on March 30, 1918, becoming known as the Battle of Moreuil Wood. A mounted squadron under the command of Lieutenant Gordon Flowerdew encountered two entrenched lines of German infantry and machine guns. Flowerdew led a mounted charge across both lines, then turned and charged again—all the way through a crossfire from machine guns. Despite seventy per cent casualties, Flowerdew and the remnants of the squadron then held the position against German counterattacks until relief arrived. Of the 150 horses in the charge, only four survived. Flowerdew died of his wounds the next day, and was posthumously awarded the Victoria Cross for his gallantry.

While hundreds of thousands of horses died during

World War I, relatively few would have been pure or predominately Canadian. Undoubtedly there were some, partly because Valcartier, the main army training centre and remount facility, was close to Quebec City. As it had during the Boer War, this proximity would have favoured horse procurement in the immediate region. Indeed, early in the war Valcartier routinely accommodated 7,000 to 8,000 horses waiting for transport to the war overseas.

Only 110 of the thousands and thousands of horses sent off to World War I ever returned to Canada. These horses belonged to senior officers. The Canadian government sold 24,000 others to the Belgian government rather than absorb the expense of bringing them home, and the Belgians auctioned them off, most likely to slaughterhouses.

The main reason only a few of the horses shipped overseas would be Canadians could be summed up in one word: scarcity. The decline in numbers had become so drastic that the government interceded to try to preserve the breed.

Chapter 9
A Dying Breed

Even at the time of Confederation, many agricultural leaders believed that pure Canadian horses no longer existed. This was an extreme view but close enough to the truth.

In 1865, for example, a prize was offered at the Sherbrooke Horse Fair for the best Canadian. Twenty-two horses were entered. In the unanimous opinion of the judges not one of the horses qualified as pure.

Almost from that time, attempts were made to "resurrect" the "old Canadian." Two approaches prevailed. The first was to breed such Canadians as remained with similar horses imported from Europe, notably with Percherons. The second was to carefully interbreed the purest Canadians available, in the hope of eventually capturing in the offspring the qualities of the originals.

Mistakes were made with the first approach. Several Percherons were imported in 1866 and 1867, but they were the wrong type. Percherons of the time were of two types, one a comparatively light horse considered similar in many respects to the Canadian, and the other much heavier. Not only were those imported of the heavy variety, but they were of poor quality. That effort to improve the breed stopped almost as soon as it began. The main legacy of the effort was damage to the credibility of Percherons in both Quebec and Ontario.

The second approach had been carried out informally by some breeders in Quebec, but only in the 1880s was the groundwork laid for a systematic program of preservation and recovery, and by then the situation had gone from bad to worse.

The most important step was the creation by the Quebec provincial government of a French-Canadian Stud Book and the appointment of a commission to oversee registration of Canadians in it. These measures were a direct result of vigorous representations by Dr. J. A. Couture and Edouard Barnard, both highly respected agronomists. Barnard's stallion, Lion of Canada, was entered as Number 1 in the Stud Book, the first registered Canadian horse.

Initially, commission registrars meticulously identified each horse by sex, birth date, sire, other progeny, height, weight, markings, pedigrees, and changes in ownership. The first two volumes of registrations listed more than 1,800 horses. By 1895, however, the commission's work had become lax. Breeders formed the Canadian Horse Breeders Association to take over the work. This seemed to help, but after several years it too became less than exact. Horses were being registered that clearly did not meet the conformation or the genealogical standards demanded for Canadians.

In 1904, the Canadian government moved to have all livestock in Canada registered. Quebec was slow to respond until breeders finally came to appreciate the value of complying—lack of registration affected their wallets because unregistered animals were worth less on the market.

But by then the Association's registration of Canadian horses was in disarray. The problems, of course, had started long before. Testifying before the 1909 Parliamentary Select Standing Committee on Agriculture and Colonization, Dr. J. G. Rutherford, Canada's Veterinary Director General and Livestock Commissioner, diplomatically pointed his finger directly at the root issue:

> *A very grave mistake was made thirty years ago by well meaning but short sighted livestock reformers, who, by the introduction of stallions of many different breeds, succeeded in almost entirely*

> *destroying the identity of the native strain ("old Canadians"), and substituting for it the nondescript mongrel now far too frequently found in the stables of our French Canadian fellow citizens.*

Rutherford had already taken the registration problems to the Breeders Association at their 1907 annual meeting. His general approach had been one of concerned optimism. What was past would stay in the past; now was the time to get on with the work of cleaning up the present situation—that was his basic message. The Association agreed with him.

Standards were redefined, making them as close to those of the "old Canadian" as possible, and the Association agreed to set aside their existing Stud Book and to appoint a fresh commission to examine every horse presented for the new registration.

By early 1909 the commission had examined 2,528 horses, of which 134 males and 835 mares had been accepted and registered. Among the 2,528 horses presented, 470 had been registered in the 1886 Stud Book. Of these, only 125 were now accepted.

In 1908, prizes were again offered for best Canadian stallions and mares, this time at a St. Johns, Quebec, exhibition. To qualify, a horse had to be listed in the new Stud Book. This contest, unlike the 1865 Sherbrooke fiasco, had 120 approved entrants. The show was an encouraging success.

Rutherford had doubts that the "old Canadian" could be truly resurrected, but he believed a close approximation could be achieved; one that reflected many of the original's best qualities and might possibly even improve upon some of them. He lobbied hard for formal selective breeding among registered horses. Finally, in 1913, his goal came much closer to achievement.

In 1912 the federal government had purchased a black Canadian mare named Helene, registered as Number 49 in the new Stud Book. Just before the purchase she had been bred to a stallion named Wilfred, Number 1012. Her foal from the breeding, born in the spring of 1913, was Albert de Cap Rouge, Number 1489. Helene and Wilfred have been described as small, but Albert at maturity weighed 1,300 pounds. This horse would grow to become as important to the foundation of present-day Canadians as Figure was to Morgans. For nineteen years Albert de Cap Rouge stood at stud on government breeding farms. His pedigree can be traced through the majority of today's registered Canadians.

Albert's name derives from the site of the first government breeding facility, established at Cap Rouge in 1913. Along with Helene, the government procured a dozen other mares, carefully chosen for size, conformation, and vitality. Cap Rouge remained a working mixed farm while it grew as

Albert de Cap Rouge, main foundation stallion for modern Canadians.

a breeding station, and the Canadians were expected to put in a full day's work.

By 1919 the horses had so proliferated that Cap Rouge was overcrowded. By then another development had been identified by private breeders to the governments in Ottawa and Quebec City. Registered or otherwise, Canadians still had many different strains and sizes that had thus far defied standardization. Breeders wanted these strains narrowed down.

Arrangements were made to move the operation to 500 acres of marginal farm land at Saint-Joachim, just east of Quebec City. The Dominion Department of Agriculture footed the bill to carry out extensive improvements to the land and to construct nineteen buildings. Quite in keeping with their heritage, the Canadians at the new farm would live outside year-round, the only concession being open sheds where they could shelter from severe weather. The first twenty-three mares and two stallions arrived from Cap Rouge in 1920. They were augmented by thirty mares purchased from private Quebec breeders.

Saint-Joachim operated successfully for twenty-one years. During that time, as the breeders had hoped, thirty-eight different strains of Canadians were reduced to eight. Uniformity could now be assured.

Albert de Cap Rouge was one of the stallions originally moved to Saint-Joachim. There, as at Cap Rouge, he lived outdoors, living to the age of twenty years. Perhaps he could have lived longer had a new farm superintendent not decided the aging stallion deserved a closed stable. Gladys Mackey Beattie notes an un-sourced allegation that confinement after a lifetime outdoors may have hastened his death.

Nevertheless, Albert's progeny lived on. During the Twenties, and especially the Thirties, horses from Cap Rouge and Saint-Joachim won many championships at fairs and exhibitions throughout Quebec and Ontario. It was a team from Cap Rouge that won out over the famed Black Horse Ale Percherons in Toronto. In 1937, eighty per cent of the horses that won first and second place prizes at the Quebec

Provincial Exhibition were of Cap Rouge lineage. This was important, because their achievement showed general acceptance among breeders that somewhat larger, heavier horses than "old Canadians" were acceptable.

The breeding operation at Saint-Joachim was wound up in 1940. Mechanization had driven horses from both the farm field and the battlefield. Indeed, thanks to Henry Ford, who began mass producing tractors in 1910, by 1920 the tractor was already more prevalent on Canadian farms than were horses, and military advances on the battlefields of World War I had signalled that the horses' days were numbered in that theatre as well. In Quebec, where at the turn of the century one in five Quebeckers owned a horse, now only one in ten did.

Other factors contributed to the decision to shut down Saint-Joachim, not least the expiration of the lease for the land, but the breeding program was generally considered to have achieved its goals. There was now a solid base for continuance and expansion of the breed.

The Quebec Department of Agriculture, which had begun breeding Canadians at its Deschambault Provincial Demonstration Farm, purchased fifteen Saint-Joachim horses, later adding another mare and a stallion.

While a few breeders continued breeding the smaller, though nevertheless acceptable horses, most favoured the heavier Canadians. The smaller horses were preferred for riding and driving, and there was a market for them in the United States, where even at that time they were often mistaken for Morgans.

The Deschambault program drew some criticism because it was directed to producing horses that were not only heavier but more docile. In short, there was a concern that the Canadians' spirit would be bred out and, with that, their characteristic vitality. The concerns proved to be unfounded. The Deschambault horses were bigger, but they kept the Canadian personality. The strain of horses bred at Deschambault was named La Gorgendiere. Because the market for farm horses had long ago collapsed, all of these horses were trained for riding, eventing, and jumping. In these regards many would excel.

When the governmental breeding operations closed, first at Cap Rouge and then at Saint-Joachim, most of the Canadians were sold to private breeders. Unfortunately, many of these breeders failed to keep up their registrations or to register their foals. The number of registered Canadians again began to decline. By the 1970s, there were fewer than 400. But the breed fought back. Eventually, all new registered Canadians had to have two registered Canadian parents, but even at that many Canadians were not registered by their owners until they were sold, at which time they had to be registered if they were to be sold as Canadians. This was puzzling, since the cost of registration, DNA testing, and other prerequisites were quite nominal.

In November 1981, the Deschambault program officially closed. The horses were sold at an auction reserved for members of the Canadian Horse Breeders Association, formerly known as the French-Canadian Horse Breeders Association. This was the end of direct government involvement.

To some breeders the closure seemed like a death knell for the breed. Others felt they were best rid of government involvement. Either way, two things were clear. First, the Canadian, whether the old or the new, was again in danger of extinction, even though the government programs had staved off this prospect for decades. Second, for the Canadian horse to survive as more than a historical artifact—a stuffed museum piece like Rienzi—greater efforts would be required to keep the breed alive and vibrant. Its fate was now in private hands.

Chapter 10
The Honourable Canadian

The Canadian remains among the most influential domestic horses in the history of North America. Arguably, it is the first domestic horse breed unique to that continent. For 250 years it was to the times what Henry Ford's Model T was to the early twentieth century. But by 1980, just like the Model T, its time appeared to have passed long ago.

The Canadian is described in Bonnie Hendricks's 1995 *International Encyclopedia of Horse Breeds* as "one of the best kept secrets of the twentieth century." Concurring with Gladys Mackey Beattie, she points out that:

> *...many purebred French-Canadian horses were entered into the early stud books of the Morgan, Standardbred, and American Saddlebred. Foundation sires of these breeds were often pure Canadian or were mated to pure Canadian mares.*

Yet the Canadian was in 1980 considered an endangered rare breed.

Some breeders in Canada recognized that the secret had to be revealed. The historic importance of the horse should not fade. Rather, it should be exalted. If the breed was to survive, widespread public education had to be undertaken; appreciation had to be nurtured.

Breeders were the first to recognize that horses are still a business—a multi-billion-dollar-a-year business in Canada. In the 1980s, as later, the market demand was primarily for purpose-bred horses. All-purpose light horses, such as the Canadian, had no place in that structure unless a niche could be found. Pulling ploughs or skidding logs definitely wasn't it.

And the breeders were well aware that the breed's integrity had to be maintained. The gene pool had been muddied enough. The government farms had helped a lot to clear it but that work—and vigilance—had to continue.

These were the challenges facing Canadian breeders in the eighties. Indeed, these are the challenges still facing them thirty years later, though by now they seem less daunting, and the breeders back then had much more limited resources.

Canadian breeders had to find a more substantial market than simply selling horses amongst themselves. Although the breed had provided harness racing with some of its earliest champions, laying a foundation for an enormous industry, Standardbred trotters and pacers now dominated the racetracks, far too fast for Canadians. Rodeos might have seemed a possibility, but Canadians were not of a temperament to make it as bucking horses, nor nimble enough to be barrel racers, nor fast enough off the mark to be effective in roping events. At the serious professional level, purpose-bred horses had locked up the rodeo niche. As to providing horsemeat to the substantial European and Asian markets, that was considered a non-starter.

The horses bred and trained at Deschambault pointed the way for the breeders. These horses had been trained to the saddle and the carriage, and for both purposes were as ideal in the twentieth century as they had been in the seventeenth. This could be a viable market niche for Canadians and, indeed, the lighter horses were already attracting American buyers for these purposes before breeders took up the reins to bring the breed back from the brink of extinction.

Another potential market was in dressage. While as

A horse and rider display their dressage skills at Beckett's Creek Farms.

jumpers the Canadians might never match world-class champions, they were ideal for novice dressage riders, and there were many more students in local training facilities than there were professionals riding on the international circuit.

There were, then, some potential markets, albeit small and generally unexploited. There was also the tremendous historical value in the breed, as yet unrecognized and, apart from breeders, unknown. At first, almost individually, breeders began to address issues and opportunities.

As a people, Canadians have a reputation as being somewhat reserved. They seem reluctant to blow their own horns. Some Canadian breeders decided to put aside such qualms. They realized that some horn-blowing would be necessary—though it would, of course, be muted.

Though it took years, Canadians began to have success at carriage driving events. In 1998, Francois Bergeron and his mare Rosie won the Single Horse on Runabout Carriage Championship at Canada's premier carriage competition, the annual Canadian Carriage Driving Classic. Then, in 2000, Bergeron was back at the Classic, winning the Reserve Championship for Single Horse "On The Road" Cart. The same year, Canadian gelding Caesar, driven by owner Sue Mott, won the Advanced Singles Championship at the prestigious Jaguar Combined Driving Triple Crown.

In carriage-driving circles, one of the niche markets, Canadians were getting very favourable attention. When owner Paul Bienvenue took his team into world championship competition in Riesenback, Germany, he came away with first place in the presentation class. Canadians weren't just good at what they did, they had the elegance to look good while they did it.

Canadians also became regulars at Toronto's annual Royal Agricultural Winter Fair. In 2008 Martial Desenais's Canadian finished first in both the Carriage Racing Derby 1 and Carriage Racing Derby 2 Jumper Relay.

Roval Xno Fancy of Cherry Creek Canadians, driven by Yvonne Hillsden.

Even royalty came to again recognize the Canadian. During her 2002 Jubilee visit to Canada, Queen Elizabeth II took the opportunity to meet Brenda Pantling's Adanac, even feeding him a carrot in a photo op. As would be expected, Adanac graciously accepted the carrot as from a peer to a peer. Royalty knows royalty.

During the twenty-plus years after the closing of Deschambault, registrations of Canadians steadily climbed. Most registered Canadians were in Quebec, as would be expected, but more and more were coming from Ontario, Alberta, British Columbia, and the United States.

Appreciation for the horse was spreading, and not only among carriage drivers.

Breeders and owners capitalized on the Canadian's legendary versatility. As a novice horse for dressage training it was superb. One example is Dart, on the registry listed as Iron Horse Hill Velour j-Artagon. In 2009 Dart was named National Canadian Horse of the Year by the Canadian Horse Breeders Association, even though Dart then lived in North Virginia.

Riding Dart, sixteen-year-old Laurel Minnick won the 2009 Northern Virginia Dressage Association first level junior young rider championship. By the end of 2010, she expected, Dart would have helped take her to the third level.

That Dart was a quick but patient study of rider and dressage requirements was no surprise to many Canadian owners. Years ago breeder Alex Hayward recalled a stallion named Duke. "Duke," he said, "could be ridden by a three-year-old girl with no bridle, just a halter with binder twine, and no saddle. He could be ridden wherever she wished."

As to the Canadian's versatility, Hayward had another memory. "Once I said they could do anything but dance. Then Ginny Dailey, who was with Park Safari, took six Canadian horses to the Royal Winter Fair. And they danced, performing at liberty, with no ill effects."

Speaking of her Canadian, Caesar, Sue Mott noted other characteristics of the breed. "One of the things that give my horse the extra edge is his power and the controllability of it. I can open him up when I need it then suddenly pull him up and he will cool right down and carry on steadily. He does not get wound up. If we get in trouble in a hazard, he does not get upset or panic. That enables us to work together and get out of trouble."

All of these qualities were put to good use in the Alberta foothills and in British Columbia's rugged interior. The strong, imperturbable Canadians came to be used as mountain horses, as saddle and pack horses for extended trail rides, and in small scale-ranching.

With the help of breeders and owners the Canadian horse was re-inventing itself to fit in with changing demands and changing times. It was not about to trot quietly into the sunset. Nevertheless, it was still relatively unknown to the wider Canadian public.

Breeders in the provincial chapters of the Canadian Horse Breeders Association, notably those in Ontario, British Columbia, and Alberta, embarked on promotional and public education activities. Rarely was an opportunity missed—exhibitions, parades, fairs, children's wagon rides at small community picnics and other public gatherings; owners would trailer in their horses to show them off. They were not there to sell horses; they were there to inform the public.

In one such effort, the Upper Canada District (Ontario) Horse Breeders Association produced 5,000 copies of a colouring book about the Canadian, which members distributed for free. The books were snapped up quicker than a new novel from Stephen King, and the Association has plans to reissue it as soon as they can find the money to cover the costs.

The Upper Canada Heritage Village in southeastern Ontario keeps a small number of Canadians. Not only are these popular attractions for the thousands of tourists who annually visit the Village, the horses are worked daily, carrying out the same chores asked of their ancestors in the early nineteenth century.

Hollywood North movie and TV producers, including Walt Disney Productions, used Upper Canada Village as movie sets, and the Canadians always managed to charm their way onto the screen. Despite that continuing success, "Legend of the Canadian Horse," a full-length documentary by Rick Blackburn would be the first time a Canadian would have a starring role. In 2009 Blackburn, to raise awareness for the breed, rode his Canadian Hannah and led his Canadian pack horse Galopin (and a cameraman) from the Plains of Abraham in Quebec to Bryan, Texas. Following the original route of French traders down the length of the United States, he was delivering fifty DNA samples from Canadian horses to Dr. Gus Cothran, Director of the Equine Genetics Research Facility at Texas A&M University, inspiring dozens of interviews and newspaper articles along the way. The DNA samples are being used in scientific studies to help determine the extent of Canadian influence on North American horse bloodlines. The documentary would raise awareness of the breed with a wide, general audience.

While, of course, Canadian breeders always had to have an eye on the marketplace, most were also constantly aware that they were entrusted with the preservation of a living, historic, national treasure. Moreover, they were also aware that their task remained an uphill climb.

They certainly found that to be the case in the nineties, when several breeders dipped into political waters with hopes of having the Canadian officially proclaimed Canada's national horse, which only an Act of Parliament could achieve.

Two of the first breeders to propose this to their local Members of Parliament lived in Dunrobin on the outskirts of Ottawa. Although breeders had tossed around the idea for years, it wasn't until Donnie Prosperine and Alex Hayward began earnestly pursuing it at the political level in 1994 that it began to draw attention.

They had acquired their Canadians from the Deschambault closure. As well, Alex Hayward was the nephew of George Atkins, who had been the foreman/manager at Saint-Joachim from the day it opened until the last horse departed. Safe to say, the two men knew Canadians. In the years that followed they would also come to know politicians. Prosperine and Hayward embarked on a mission that would require tireless lobbying of the federal Members of Parliament and Senators.

Quickly they discovered that they first had to educate the politicians as to why the Canadian was so important and so deserving of a place as a symbol of Canada. They became regulars on Parliament Hill, often showing up in a splendid carriage drawn by an equally splendid team of Canadians.

A Private Member's Bill seemed the best way to get the campaign to the House of Commons, even though such bills usually died before a vote was taken. Prosperine, Hayward, and their supporters had to find a Member of Parliament willing to front the bill.

The first to accept the challenge, in 1995, was Ontario MP Ian Murray. The House declared his bill non-votable, and didn't even send it to committee. MP Murray Calder was the next convert. MP Calder raised chickens, and the nearest thing to a horse on his farm was a pet Bactrian camel named Baxter, but he became convinced of the importance of recognizing the Canadian breed. He proposed a Bill in 1998, but it died when parliament shut down for an election.

In 1999, determined, he tried again. Recognition for the Canadian seemed a harmless issue, a slam dunk—who could object?

As it turned out, Westerners, Newfoundlanders, the Bloc Québécois, the Reform Party, and the NDP were all moved to object. An MP from the West said the Canadian had had nothing to do with settling Western Canada and thus could not be representative of the nation as a whole. He also thought the bill was an insult to prairie Native peoples. After discovering that he was wrong on both counts, he eventually did vote for the bill. A member for Newfoundland felt that the Newfoundland pony, though little-known off the island, was more deserving of the honour—or, at least, of a share. The Bloc said it was just one more attempt to usurp and assimilate Québécois history and culture, it was a frivolous waste of the Members' time, and anyway the Bloc's provincial counterpart, the Parti Québécois, had just passed a unanimous resolution in the provincial assembly that the Canadian was Quebec's official horse.

With so many voices against it, the bill seemed doomed. A Private Member's Bill needs unanimous support in the House, and Reform, the NDP, and the Bloc were determined to vote against this one. Three attempts were made to get a bill passed in the House, and all three failed.

But the Canadian's supporters didn't give up. Instead, breeders across the country took up the cause, and descended upon their local MPs. Yvonne Hillsden, a prominent British Columbia breeder, was joined by many others in the West. Veterinarian Dr. Kelly Ferguson, who owned a team of Canadians, enlisted the support of her neighbour, Senator Lowell Murray—which was easy enough, since he was already on record as supporting the Calder bill.

In 2001, Dr. Ferguson approached Senator Murray with an unorthodox proposal. Would he introduce a Private Member's Bill in the Senate? Murray agreed. Hearings were held, experts testified, the Senators were convinced, and the bill S-22 was passed and forwarded to the House of Commons.

With the Senate's having given its approval, and the cause's supporters continuing their judicious lobbying of MPs, victory for the Canadian was near. It took a bit of last-minute manoeuvring (including, according to one source, a nudge from long-time eastern Ontario MP Don Boudria) to get Prime Minister Jean Chrétien to agree to put it on the Order Paper, but the bill eventually passed first reading, went to the Standing Committee on Canadian Heritage, and came back to the House for final approval. On April 30, 2002, Bill S-22 received royal assent. The Canadian was now the national horse of Canada.

That night, doubtless, Canadian horses from the Atlantic to the Pacific received a few extra oats and, for some, a few extra apples and carrots. In a sense they were once again royalty, though it had taken 335 years. There was one sad note, however. Donnie Prosperine, who had worked so tirelessly to have the Canadian become recognized as Canada's National Horse, died shortly before the Bill's successful passage.

In 2009, the Canadian received an additional honour

when it appeared on a commemorative postage stamp.

Honours aside, the day-to-day lives of the horses continued much as usual. Registrations, which had climbed to nearly 6,000, slowed somewhat with the global economic downturn after 2008. Breeders also experienced dramatically reduced horse sales, likely for the same reason.

Canadians remain a rare breed. Equine Canada estimated there were 950,000 horses in the country in 2010, but only 0.6 per cent were registered Canadians. Nevertheless, they hold the most honoured position of any horse breed in Canada. And the breeders are firm: the Canadians are here to stay.

Acknowledgements

Many of the people who have contributed to this book are long-time owners, trainers, and breeders of Canadian horses. For each of those who have helped me are a dozen more I wanted to contact but couldn't due to time constraints. However, some day I hope to rectify these omissions.

Alone and by any of its various names, the influential role of the Canadian horse in shaping Canada's history warrants recognition of the breed as Canada's official national horse. Add to that the breed's role in the genesis of almost all other important North American horse breeds and its stature as our premier horse becomes profound. Recognizing this is perhaps the best acknowledgement I can provide.

Further Reading

Beattie, Gladys Mackey. *The Canadian Horse: A Pictorial History*. North Hatley, P.Q., 1981.

Briggs, Karen. "Northern Exposure: Breed Profile." *Horse Illustrated*: November, 2005.

Christman, Carolyn J. et al. *A Rare Breeds Album of American Livestock*. Pittsboro, North Carolina: The American Livestock Breeds Conservancy, 1998.

Dohner, Janet Vorwald. *The Enyclopedia of Historic and Endangered Livestock and Poultry Breeds*. New Haven: Yale University Press, 2001.

First Session, Eleventh Parliament. "Report of the Select Standing Committee on Agriculture and Colonization." *House of Commons*. Ottawa: King's Printer, 1909.

Jones, Robert Leslie. "The Old French-Canadian Horse: Its History in Canada and the United States." *The Canadian Historical Review*, Vol. XXVIII, No.2: June, 1947.

Scanlan, Lawrence. *Little Horse of Iron*. Toronto: Vintage Press, 2002.

Staff, The Beaver. "Can, Huh? Duh? – The Little Iron Horse." *The Beaver*, Vol.1, No. 4: August/September, 2005.

Wilson, Barry. "Canada trots toward national horse." *Western Producer*: March 7, 2002.

Illustration Credits

The photograph on the front cover of this book shows Swallowfielfd Eno Kelbeck #8572 ("Kal"), a black Canadian stallion. The image is reproduced by permission of the photographer, Deb Harper of Abbotsford, B.C..

Images on the following pages appear courtesy of the following sources:

p. 10, Brenda Pantling, Hidden Meadow Farms; p. 16, Cornelius Krieghoff, "Habitant Sleigh, View Near the Canadian Line," c. 1847; p. 26, Patti and Shane Juuti, West Gimlet Farms; p. 40, Cornelius Krieghoff, "Sleigh Race on the St. Lawrence at Quebec," 1852; p. 42, Cornelius Krieghoff, "Breaking up of a Country Ball in Canada, Early Morning (the Morning After a Merrymaking in Lower Canada)," 1857; p. 63, Patti and Shane Juuti, West Gimlet Farms; p. 67, Library and Archives Canada, C-073720; p. 79, Patti and Shane Juuti, West Gimlet Farms; p. 93, Library and Archives Canada, C-027589; p. 104, Yvonne Hillsden, Cherry Creek Canadians; p. 112, Ray Lalonde, Beckett's Creek Farms; p. 114, Yvonne Hillsden, Cherry Creek Canadians.

About the Author

Canadian Arthur (Art) Montague began writing professionally in the year 2000. After living in Ottawa for more than two decades, he has recently retired, with his family in tow, to the historic community of Perth, Ontario, where he continues to write about those things which matter to him. History, crime, and biography are foremost in his interests.

His non-fiction includes four popular histories in the Amazing Stories series: *Canada's Rumrunners, Crime Boss Killings, Disasters Across Canada,* and *Meyer Lansky.* In 2007 he edited a quasi-travel guide entitled *The Ottawa Book of Everything* (MacIntyre-Purcell Publishing), and has over 200 feature articles and essays in print and Internet publications.

Montague was drawn to the fascinating story of the Canadian Horse while reviewing 2001 Hansard transcripts of the spirited debate among MPs on the question of the horse's national recognition. Following the passage of Bill S-22, April 30, 2002, which established the Canadian Horse as Canada's national horse, he researched and wrote an article entitled "Breed History of the Canadian Horse" for the *Equine Literary Journal.* Montague's feature article "A Horse Fit for a Country" appears in the 2011 issue of *The Old Farmer's Almanac,* Canadian edition.

Index